THE LEGEND OF GRIZZLY ADAMS

A Kid on the Comstock: Reminiscences
of a Virginia City Childhood
John Taylor Waldorf

The Story of the Mine
Charles Howard Shinn

Karnee: A Paiute Narrative
Lalla Scott

Will James: The Last Cowboy Legend
Anthony Amaral

The Legend of Grizzly Adams:
California's Greatest Mountain Man
Richard H. Dillon

BOOKS BY RICHARD H. DILLON

Embarcadero

The Gila Trail

Shanghaiing Days

California Trail Herd

The Hatchet Men

Meriwether Lewis

J. Ross Browne: Confidential Agent in Old California

Fool's Gold: The Decline and Fall of
Captain John Sutter of California

Humbugs and Heroes: A Gallery of California Pioneers

Burnt-out Fires

Siskiyou Trail: The Hudson's Bay Company
Route to California

Images of Chinatown:
Louis J. Stellman's Chinatown Photographs

We Have Met the Enemy:
Oliver Hazard Perry, Wilderness Commodore

Delta Country: Narrative

North American Indian Wars

Indian Wars, 1850-1890

Wells, Fargo Detective: A Biography of James B. Hume

Texas Argonauts: Isaac H. Duval
and the California Gold Rush

The Legend of Grizzly Adams:
California's Greatest Mountain Man

THE LEGEND
OF
GRIZZLY ADAMS:

California's Greatest Mountain Man

RICHARD H. DILLON

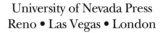

University of Nevada Press
Reno • Las Vegas • London

To David Magee
Britannic bibliopole of San Francisco

Acknowledgments

I am indebted for aid and counsel to many people but particularly to
Carlo DeFerrari, Allan R. Ottley, Francis Farquhar, Dr. Al Shumate,
Dorothy Firebaugh and Ruby E. Hult.

RHD

Vintage West Series Editor: Robert E. Blesse

The Legend of Grizzly Adams: California's Greatest Mountain Man by Richard H. Dillon was
originally published by Coward-McCann, Inc., of New York, in 1966. The University of
Nevada Press edition reproduces the original except for the front matter, which has
been modified to reflect the new publisher, and a new paperback cover.

The Legend of Grizzly Adams is reprinted with the kind permission of
Bulls on the Run Productions, Inc.

The paper used in this book meets the requirements of American
National Standard for Information Sciences—Permanence of Paper
for Printed Library Materials, ANSI Z39.48-1984. Binding
materials were selected for strength and durability.

Library of Congress Cataloging-in-Publication Data
Dillon, Richard H.
The legend of Grizzly Adams, California's greatest mountain man /
Richard H. Dillon.
p. cm. — (Vintage West series)
Originally published: New York : Coward-McCann, 1966.
ISBN 0-87417-207-1 (alk. paper)
1. Adams, Grizzly, 1812-1860. 2. Hunters—California—Biography.
3. Trappers—California—Biography. I. Title. II. Series.
F864.A39D54 1993
639'.1'092—dc20
[B]   92-39768
CIP

University of Nevada Press, Reno, Nevada 89557 USA
Copyright © 1966 by Richard H. Dillon
All rights reserved
Cover design by Ann Lowe
Printed in the United States of America

2 4 6 8 9 7 5 3 1

CONTENTS

Illustrations after pps. 96 and 160

INTRODUCTION

MYSTERY MAN

T HE greatest California mountain man of them all was Grizzly Adams. He was also one of the most mysterious men in the history of the Far West. For some reason still hidden to us, he chose to use the aliases William Adams and James Capen Adams, the latter his brother's name, although he was born John Adams.

Did he have a brush with the law? If so, it is not in the existing records. Was he ashamed of his reversion to near-Indian savagery in the wilderness? Did he consider himself (a failure as both family man and businessman) to be the black sheep of the whole New England Adams clan which was so productive of great writers, philosophers and Presidents of the United States? But if he sought to truly hide his identity, why did he cling to Adams rather than calling himself James Smith or J. C. Jones? All of these are questions without answers. Perhaps the key lies locked in the mystery of the suicide of his father, Eleazar, by hanging at Charlton, Massachusetts, where Grizzly chose to be buried, though he was born in Medway and died in Neponset. Was there not a connection between his father's taking his own life on June 5, 1849, and Grizzly's departure for California that year?

What we *do* know about Old Adams, or Bruin Adams, as he was sometimes called, is considerable. He had a complete and marvelous disregard for convention. He was the most nonconformist of all Adamses. Excluding such wild eccentrics as Oofty-Goofty and Emperor Norton, he was probably the greatest individualist that California ever produced. And California, from John Sutter's time onward, never had individualists in short supply. Unfortunately for historians, if not for readers, Adams also had an almost complete disregard for the truth. Or, at least, he was hard put to distinguish between fact and fiction. It is not that Grizzly dissimulated for gain. He was not even a deliberate liar. He simply could not resist improving upon a true incident in the telling and retelling. He should have been a novelist, not a bear tamer. In this respect, of course, he differed little from most of the other great mountain men of the West, all of whom—Davy Crockett, Jim Beckwourth, Jim Bridger, etc.—apparently drank too deeply of the waters of the Hassayampa. In any case, Adams resolutely refused to let facts stand in the way of a good story. His amanuensis of a century ago, Theodore H. Hittell, found his memory to be remarkable—unfading, in fact. But later writers, like the undersigned, have found it more chameleon-like than amaranthine. For example, in one account his hunting companion on a particular expedition will be called Drury; in another account, Carroll; and in a third, Brown. Adventures, most of which really happened, are placed, replaced and misplaced geographically in the many hops, skips and stumbles of his memory. On his deathbed, Adams himself confessed to the person in attendance that he was a spinner of tall tales. But he never admitted to lapses of memory.

While Adams was not of great physical stature, he was wiry, and strong as a percheron. Outstanding among his characteristics was his reckless courage. He was braver than Kit Carson or Jim Savage, the White King of the Tulare Indians. He loved to tackle an angry grizzly, a claim few men—even mountain men—dared to put forward. He was also a loner.

He was more completely at home in the wilds than the most rugged *coureur de bois* or *métis engagé* of the upper Missouri. Adams was satisfied with the companionship of grizzly bears and, perhaps, a dog. Incredibly, he actually preferred the company of Indians to whites, animals to Indians, and wild beasts to domesticated pets.

But what most set Adams apart from John Sutter, Caleb Greenwood or Peter Lassen, or a half-dozen other pioneers of the West Coast wilderness, was not his valor or self-sufficiency but his unique domination over the "horrible bear" (*Ursus horribilis*) or ferocious bear (*Ursus ferox*), the dreaded, fearless grizzly bear. From this first description of the animals by Meriwether Lewis in 1804, hunters and trappers preferred to give them a wide berth. Of them Captain Lewis wrote: "These bears, being so hard to die, rather intimidate us all. I must confess that I do not like the gentleman and had rather fight two Indians than one grizzly bear." Adams was a braggart but, strangely, he never made much out of the strange power he possessed. He just dismissed the matter of his sway over the brutes by observing of his wild animal menagerie that he himself was "the hardest animal in the collection."

The Wild Yankee, in telling the story of his life and adventures, could not resist romanticizing even his birth. He told Hittell that he was born under a great pine tree while his father was laboriously cutting and splitting timber into logs and puncheons for a rude cabin in the Aroostook wilderness of the Maine frontier. Jokingly, he located the exact spot for his interviewer by saying it was where the Down Easters of legend had the solemn duty of winding up the sun, each dawn, with a windlass. Hittell did not realize from this joke that the whole story was just one of Grizzly's tall tales, and he swallowed it as gospel. The Adams family genealogist was more discerning and he put it kindly but plainly when he said of Adams's autobiography: "It has been impossible to verify its statements or reconcile them with information from other sources."

Actually, Grizzly was born John Adams and not in a howling wilderness but in a solid and dull Massachusetts town between Boston and Worcester, on October 22, 1812. He was the third child of Eleazar Adams and Sybil Capen Adams, being preceded into the world by Susan and Almy and followed by siblings Charles, James Capen, Zilpha, Francis D. and Albert. Young John Adams was born into a well-settled, if not ancient, Massachusetts community. Medway was the sixty-ninth town to be incorporated in the Massachusetts Bay Colony and was only ninety-nine years old in the year of Adams's birth, 1812. The town was carved out of Medfield, and included all the portion lying west of the Charles River. Of the forty-eight founders of the town, eight bore the surname Adams.

For a boy of such an adventurous nature as that possessed by romantic John Adams, Medway must have seemed tame indeed. There were no lofty mountains to make the horizon jagged, only soft and gentle hills. There were no wild woods to explore, only the boggy pine patch called Black Swamp. There were no prairies and when John fished the Charles and its tributaries, Boggastow Brook, Winthrop Pond and Chicken Brook, he must have yearned for the dashing streams and tumbling waterfalls of Lewis and Clark's West, rather than the parklike country southwest of Boston.

Born too late to "enjoy" the break in the tedium of Medway life which the hurricane of 1815, the so-called Great Blow, brought, Adams spent a boyhood of quiet ranging the countryside, the nearest thing to a wilderness which the area boasted. He hunted and fished, picked cranberries in meadows and bogs, and explored Trout Brook, Long Plain and Pine Grove. The only exciting site around Medway was Dinglehole, the reputed rendezvous of witches and even Satan himself, at times, accompanied by his disciples. Around this pit, partially filled with stagnant water, strange lights were to be seen, at night, while uncanny and unearthly sounds were uttered. The hole took its name from another mysterious phenomenon, the ringing of a bell, or dingle, called the Spirit Bell, which none of the townsfolk ever saw. Worst of all—and shades òf Sleepy Hollow!—a headless man was often seen, accompanied by fireballs and witches capable of transforming themselves, at will, into coons and weasels before your very eyes!

But, Dinglehole apart, Medway was much too sedate for a boy who would, one day, be widely known as Grizzly Adams, the Wild Yankee. The old postrider's road had been improved in 1807 into the Boston and Hartford Turnpike and the jehu Joseph Miller drove the first stages into town on the Boston-Hartford run during the year Adams was born. The road was busy with traffic and the neighborhood was much too settled for Adams, but he enjoyed the diversion of the stages with their lathered horses and thundering wheels and especially the shrilling of the bugles as the drivers signaled ahead for the change of horses in Medfield.

Of course, there was much history in Medway. Richardson's Hotel was the building in which George Washington had his dinner in 1775 en route to Cambridge on the Old Mendon Road to take command of the American Army, and the old Stone House on Boggastow Pond was the bastion from which the settlers had more than once beaten off attacks during the Indian wars. Perhaps the most delightful break in the tedium of small-town life for John Adams was the celebration of Independence Day each year. When he was seven and a half or so, July 4, 1820, rolled around and it proved to be an exceptional holiday. For, that year, Medfield had a cannon brought from Walpole. The fieldpiece was placed in front of the hotel and worked by a gunner of the Walpole Artillery Company, while Medfield's militia paraded to the notes of fife and drum. There was much drinking of toasts and after each toast the cannon was fired, shaking all Medfield and Medway. John was too young to notice how shaken were the celebrants by the frequent toasts laced between cannon blasts.

The most prominent business in town came to be, during Adams's boyhood, the manufacture of boots and shoes, so it was only natural that John, as he matured, should drift into the industry. By the year of his marriage (1836), the business of shoemaking employed 300 persons and Medway was producing 40,000 pairs of boots and 100,000 pairs of shoes per year. John was born just about the time Boston was revolutionizing the bootmaking and shoemaking industry. Medway, a satellite of Boston, soon saw pegs of maple replaced by shoe nails, and lasts began to be turned by lathes rather than by hand. Before he was grown, John Adams knew the cobbler's entire lexicon and could distinguish all the various breeds of footgear, from gaiters and ladies' buskins to Negro brogans or the sheepskin children's shoes called roan butts.

With the sole exception of an unforgettable interlude of hunting and animal training in New England, during the course of which he was severely injured, Adams stuck to his lasts and endured the boring life of a bootmaker in Medway and Boston. But in 1849 he threw away his pegs and his awl and struck out for Golden California.

The story of Grizzly Adams becomes even more confused once he has emigrated to California, which is why this account of the colorful Californian's life is set down as legend rather than history or biography, although it is as accurate as research plus calculated hunches can make it. He presumably came overland, via Mexico, to try his hand at mining, ranching, storekeeping and even, swallowing his battered pride, shoemaking. He had little real success in any of these endeavors, however, and finally turned his back on civilization to make his home in the wild Sierra with the grizzlies and mountain lions.

There were Adamses aplenty in the Mother Lode during the gold rush, and mostly from Massachusetts. Not a few of them had the initial J. before their family name, too. Deciding just who is who among these New Englanders is a task which would awe Holmes and Moriarty. William E. Coutrell, who registered the citizens of Tuolumne County for the first Federal Census in California, found a Massachusetts-born Jamestown merchant on April 12, 1851, who gave his name as J. C. Adams. But was this man Grizzly Adams? Who is to say? If he was, he not only did not give his right name but used his brother's (and the real James Capen never came to California, but stayed back East to raise his seven children), and lied about his age, giving it as twenty-seven years when he was almost thirty-five years old.

So many miners were left out of the 1850 census, scattered as they were all over the mountains in dry creeks and on sandbars, that a special California State Census was conducted in 1852. Four men in Tuolumne County were identified as J. Adams but one was from Missouri, one from Vermont, and one from Pennsylvania. The fourth "J. Adams" and one "John Adams" were listed as miners from Massachusetts, thirty-seven years old and twenty-four years old, respectively. The first man may very well have been our Grizzly, for he was either thirty-six or thirty-seven years old. But how about the "John Adams" located in 1852 in San Joaquin County? He was a Massachusetts-born shoemaker! But he gave his age as thirty-two, instead of thirty-six or thirty-seven. Could it have been old forgetful John (Grizzly) Adams?

On March 7, 1853, M. B. Duffield deeded a ranch to a J. C. Adams—"that certain lot, piece, or parcel of land situate (sic) in Tuolumne County, state of California, about sixteen miles east of the city of Sonora and about one-half mile west of Sugar Pine Creek, being between the said creek and the Stanislaus River." Now, this certainly sounds like our J. C. Adams because this is his stamping ground as a bear hunter

—the upper reaches of the Stanislaus, Tuolumne and Merced rivers. The property would, today, be near Long Barn or just west of Pinecrest. Ten miles to the east lay Strawberry Ranch, to which Grizzly referred several times in his memoirs. Prior to coming to Tuolumne County, Grizzly Adams owned a ranch on the San Joaquin River near French Camp but borrowed money on it, could not repay the loan, and lost the property. A born bad businessman, Adams went broke in Tuolumne County, too.

But there was another J. C. Adams in the Sierra foothills in the decade of 1850–1860. On March 3, 1860, Frederick Salter deeded land on the north branch of Turnback Creek to a man by that name. And Grizzly Adams on that date was far out at sea (having sailed on the clipper *Golden Fleece* from San Francisco for New York on January 7, 1860) or, possibly, he was just-arrived in the metropolis. Further, the recipient of the property signed himself John C. Adams. The mystery was finally cleared up when, on December 17, 1862 —long after Grizzly was dead—this J. C. Adams deeded the Turnback Creek property to William Peters and finally signed his full name—John Connor Adams.

Once he headed for the Sierra headwaters of the Tuolumne and its fellow streams, we have a good idea of Adams's strange career, right up to the moment of his death in the bosom of his family (his wife, Sybil, and children Arabella, Arathusa Elizabeth, and Seymour) at Neponset in 1860. Real fame came to him in New York, when he joined forces with Phineas T. Barnum and J. M. Nixon, of Niblo's Garden, and opened the California Menagerie on April 30, 1860, at the corner of 13th Street and Fourth Avenue. Two days before the opening, the theatrical and sporting paper, the *New York Clipper*, predicted that "those among our fellow citizens who are partial to 'roaring amusements' will doubtless be on hand."

On May 5th, *Wilke's Spirit of the Times* carried an advertisement for the Californian's wild animal show in which Grizzly modestly promised potential patrons "the most curious, unique, and interesting museum of animated nature ever presented to the public." By the following Monday, Adams's name was known to New Yorkers from Fort Tryon to the Battery. For at 10 o'clock he led off a great parade— "a grand caravan procession"—by the side of his pack bear, both of them on a special car followed by a band chariot. The procession moved down Broadway to Park, thence up Chatham Street and Third Avenue to a firm place in New York, as well as California, history and legend.

Grizzly Adams's life is, most of all, a grand story. But he was more than a mere colorful, idiosyncratic personality in the passing parade. There are those who swear that artist Charles Nahl's drawings of one of his bears were the basis for the design of California's state flag. (Nahl was the artist who worked with Hittell on Grizzly's 1860 autobiography.) But more important, zoological gardens were established at both ends of the continent as a result, in part, of the example of Adams and his wild animal menageries. In San Francisco, his Mountaineer Museum was followed by Woodward's Gardens and, eventually, the splendid Fleishhacker Zoo of today. New York's great zoo is in the Bronx, of course, rather than in Central Park or elsewhere in Manhattan but, once again, its founding owes something to the initial impetus provided by Grizzly Adams's California Menagerie of 1860.

On June 23, 1860, *Wilke's Spirit of the Times* published an editorial under the head, "Shall We Have Zoological Gardens?": "We trust the project for the establishment of zoological gardens in Central Park of this metropolis will be persecuted with vigor.... No gathering exists of the beasts and birds of our own native land.... Just look at the collection made by the old Rocky Mountain hunter, Adams, and then see what might be done with means and science. He has

17

gotten together some eight or nine varieties of the American bear, from the monstrous grizzly of the size of an ox down to the little golden bear."

Grizzly Adams lived a full life. He died with courage and wry humor, proud of having bamboozled P. T. Barnum. He is said to have stated on his deathbed, "I have looked on death in many forms and I trust that I can meet it whenever it comes, with a stout heart and steady nerves." His only regret was that he did not see the last set of the sun in the company of his old ursine friends, Ben and Lady Washington, in the Sierra he loved so much, saying, "There, surely, I could find rest through the long future among the eternal rocks and evergreen pines."

RICHARD DILLON

San Francisco

THE LEGEND OF GRIZZLY ADAMS:
California's Greatest Mountain Man

CHAPTER I

MOUNTAIN MAN

Early one sunny morning in the fall of 1852, a wiry, muscular man yoked two oxen to a battered old wagon and geed and hawed them along the road out of the river port of Stockton. He headed east toward the granite which still hid the rays of the rising sun. The drover's name was John Adams. He sometimes called himself Yankee Adams but was best known in California as J. C. Adams or James Capen Adams, which was not his name at all, but that of one of his younger brothers. He was a mystery man as well as a mountain man who wore his hair long and his face bristling with a heavy beard and moustache. Since his hair was beginning to turn gray—although he was only forty years old—his few friends of the Mother Lode and Sierra foothills were already beginning to call him Old Adams. Within a few months, he would be famous all over the Southern Mines and eventually well known throughout California as Grizzly Adams.

For all of his bushy beard, John Adams was old neither in years or spirit. Jouncing about in the wagon behind him was his blanket roll, also some old clothes, a few bowie knives and a handful of tools. Laid out carefully atop the blanket where he could get at them quickly, if necessary, were two rifles. One was an old Kentucky rifle which used thirty balls to a pound of lead. Beside it lay a long, lean, Tennessee rifle whose bullets measured sixty to the pound. On the heavy leather belt buckled around Adams's waist hung a holstered Colt revolver. This was about all the property in the world which Adams owned after a quarter century of hard work. And he was voluntarily abandoning all hope of getting any more. Litigation had stripped him of his money and his San Joaquin County ranch on the river near French Camp. He had borrowed money on his land, been unable to pay, and had had the property taken away from him. In this affair Adams also lost his faith in mankind. Looking back in 1860 to his migration to the Sierra, he recalled, "I found myself without a cent. I was dead broke. The lawyers and the judges in the course of certain differences and settlements between us, contrived to rob me of everything I possessed. . . . I was disgusted with my fellow men and their hypocrisy, their betrayal of confidence, their treachery and fraud."

As the oxen plodded along the dusty track toward the mountains, Adams thought back on the life he had lived, the life on which he was turning his back. He was through with cities and civilization—and particularly with so-called "civilized" people. He snorted as he muttered the word, then spat into the ruts in disgust. Reflecting on his forty years of life, he wondered how on earth he had managed to squander so many years so quickly. Since his birth, back in the Norfolk County town of Medway, Massachusetts * on October 22, 1812, he had tried city life and country life, shoemaking, hunting, business, mining and farming. And what had it

---

* According to his 1856 narration to Thomas H. Hittell in San Francisco, Medway was, indeed, his birthplace but the forgetful or fibbing mountaineer gave his birthdate as October 20, 1807. In his 1860 dictation to an anonymous hack, at the behest of P. T. Barnum who wanted some publicity on his new discovery (Adams), Grizzly claimed that he was born in the disputed Territory of Maine near the Aroostook River and first saw the light of day in May 1805. Albert Johannsen, not citing his source, stated in his *The House of Beadle and Adams* (University of Oklahoma, 1950) that Adams was born near Seneca Lake, New York.

22

gotten him? He twisted around to look into the wagon bed
... one bedroll, one Kentucky rifle, one Tennessee rifle. ...
Again he spat over the side of the vehicle, growling like a
grizzly to himself in disgust. He goaded his oxen on with a
volley of curses. Sorry beasts they were, just what his shambles
of a wagon deserved. He later described his outfit: "The oxen
couldn't rise when they lay down unless I lifted them by the
tail." Of the wagon, he added, "It wouldn't hold together
if I didn't soak it for a week."

But as Adams began to leave the oaks and ash behind,
their growing-naked branches signaling the approach of winter, his spirits brightened. Traffic on the road began to thin
out. This he liked. The route became more winding, rough
and steep as the oxen put more miles between their tails and
the banks of the San Joaquin River. Finally, the deciduous
trees and grassland were replaced by smoky Digger pines and
chaparral, or buckbrush. Then California's native holly—
toyon—began to appear, accompanied by small-leaved man-
zanita and other bushes of higher altitude. Rustlings in the
brush told him of the movements of small animals spying
on his passage. The air seemed clearer and fresher than in
the Great Valley. As his spirits rose, Adams began to calmly
contrast, to balance out, the good times of his life with the
bad. His first mistake, he mused, had been allowing his parents to make a shoemaker out of him when he was a boy in
New England. Or, rather, *trying* to make one of him. He
had known, even as a lad, that he was not cut out for routine
of any kind and especially not the boring life of a cobbler's
bench.

Adams remembered with what relief he had tossed aside
the hammer and pegging awl on his twenty-first birthday.
There had followed that wonderful period of his life when
he had done exactly as he liked—and was paid for it. Hired
by a company of showmen, he had scoured the forests of
Maine, Vermont and New Hampshire for wild animals to

trap and exhibit in the cities—wildcats, panthers, wolves, foxes. ... Then fate had stepped in. The owners of the menagerie to which he sold his catch, placing great faith in his strange power over wild animals, asked him to quiet an unruly Bengal tiger. Adams would never forget that day. He bore souvenirs of it still, in the form of scars on his body. He had entered the cage several times, cowing the tiger with his courage. But on his last exit, as he turned away, the yellow-eyed, treacherous cat pounced upon him, mauling him terribly with teeth and claws. Memory of that day was a nightmare of pain, crunching fangs and raking talons. The show folk had dragged his body from the cage, more dead than alive. But, and he grinned as he thought of it, Old Adams had fooled them! Even in his twenties, he had proved to be as tough as a dragoon's boot. The cat was not born, even yet, which could kill Grizzly Adams.

Painful though the memories were, he recalled them to mind. He remembered how he had slowly regained his health and strength after recovery seemed impossible. But a life of hunting was out of the question. There was only one thing to do; refusing to become a burden to his parents, he returned to the hated life of a bootmaker. Luckily, the injuries to his spine had not paralyzed his hands so he was able to set himself up in Boston in his old trade again. And he had worked hard. For fifteen long years he had bent over soles and lasts and heels, tapping and cutting and polishing. At the end of that time, Adams, being a thrifty Yankee, had saved between $6,000 and $8,000.

As he wound up into the foothills of the Sierra Nevada, Adams cast his thoughts back to that critical day, only four years behind him, the day on which he had decided to try to run this comfortable nest egg into a fortune. He had shrewdly figured that the thousands of men going west to Missouri and Kansas and Oregon—and fabled California— needed shoes and boots more than anything except perhaps flour, whiskey and guns. So, he had bought footgear to the last penny of his savings and had sent them to St. Louis with the hope of doubling or tripling his capital. Instead, he had lost every cent of his investment in a fire.

This blow had decided him to head for California. He had nothing—literally nothing—to lose. The city life of Boston did not appeal to him. The news of Jim Marshall's discovery of gold in Sutter's millrace at Coloma excited him. Soon an attack of gold fever was raging in his system. He rationalized that, even if he could not regain a fortune, he would be able to hunt and trap, again, in that wild country. Since he had no money, he could not take ship from Boston to San Francisco. However, his roving inclinations were better suited, in any case, by the overland route. He would not have liked the confinement and boredom of a clipper ship passage around Cape Horn. So he had joined a party setting out for El Dorado via Mexico and the Gila Trail through Arizona.

It had been a memorable journey. In Chihuahua City, the capital of Mexico's frontier state, he had got sick and had been left, supposedly dying, by his companions. Too tough to die, Adams had recovered and joined another train of emigrants only to fall ill again in Los Angeles. Here, again, he was left to die by his comrades but once again pulled through, thanks to his casehardened constitution.

In the next three years, Adams had tried everything and everything had gone wrong, whether mining, trading, ranching or stock raising. He had occasionally been rich but was usually poor. At his ranch at French Camp, near Stockton, a fine spread on which he had grazed a herd of cattle worth thousands of dollars, almost every head had been rustled in a single night. Other farmlands and mining claims had gotten away from him because of the double-dealing of men whom he had trusted. And his own reckless, gambling speculation was also responsible for his poverty. In those three short years in California he had tried prospecting, mining (even hiring men to dig for him) and running a grocery store and board-inghouse near Sonora. He had gone from wealth right back to indigence three times over. He was as penniless in 1852 as he had been in 1849 or on the day his father, Eleazer, first took him to the bootmaker in Massachusetts to learn a trade.

Finally, he had resolved to turn to the wilds again. The days he had spent as a hunter in New England were the finest of his life. He had given himself a taste of this life again, bear hunting in 1851, and he found that he had lost none of his appetite for it. In September of that year he had run into the British traveler Frank Marryat on a Concord coach en route to Sonora from Stockton. The Britisher had questioned him closely about his wild life. Adams would have been amused to find himself in Marryat's book, *Mountains and Molehills,* just three years after he rode toward the Sierra. Wrote Marryat: "We had one decided character. This was a man who, as he gratuitously informed us, was professionally a bear hunter, bear trapper, and bear fighter; who, in fact, dealt generally in grizzly bears. When he shot bears—and it appeared he lived in the mountains—he sold the meat and cured the skins. But when he was fortunate enough to trap a fine grizzly alive, a rich harvest generally awaited him. The grizzly was immediately transferred, bound head and foot, to a large and strong cage; and this being mounted on the bed of a wagon, the animal was dispatched to some large mining town in the vicinity, where notice was given by means of handbills and posters that 'on the Sunday following, the famous grizzly bear America, would fight a wild bull.' "

As he rode into the wilderness, Adams resolved that from now on, he would forsake the accumulation of money. Wealth was a curse. He would live the life he wanted, wandering, hunting and fishing, beholden to no one. The wilderness would be his home, wild animals his companions. He would become not a hermit, of Biblical cut, but a Robinson Crusoe of the Sierra.

When he reached a spot about sixteen miles east of Sonora, on the piney ridge between the Tuolumne River's North Fork and the Stanislaus River, he decided to stop. He halted his oxen, got down his ax and began to build a log hut. He was about half a mile west of Sugar Pine Creek, between that stream and the Stanislaus, just about on the site of present-day Long Barn.*

* Adams's always-hazy memory played tricks on him when he tried to recall the exact site of his Sierra camp. Eventually, he was not sure whether he built a log hut or lived in a *parfleche* tepee! But in the spring of 1853, using what money he had saved and received from hides and furs, etc., he bought the land on which he squatted from M. B. Duffield for $2,100. The date was March 7, 1853. Adams may have camped, first, farther upstream and returned to this site to set down roots; in various accounts he gives the headwaters of the Merced—*and the Tuolumne*—as his campsite. And one of his ghostwriters misheard him and located him at the headwaters of the (nonexistent) Tinco River.

CHAPTER II

WASHINGTON TERRITORY

ALL of the mountain country looked good to Adams. The air was perfumed with the fragrance of pine needles; their duff made a soft carpet underfoot. His rifle brought him all the provisions he needed. There was pasturage for his oxen at the very side of the trail. Evergreens and granite rocks and clear Sierra air acted like a tonic on him, allowing him to throw off all his cares and memories of earlier disappointments. No white men were in the area but Adams fell in with a tribe of so-called Digger Indians and quickly made friends with them.

Being a dead shot, it was child's play for Adams to kill deer for the Indians. He used his rifle to fill their stomachs. They loved venison but their bows and arrows were more likely to supply them with rabbits and other small fare, rather than deer. Their normal diet ran mainly to fish, nuts, acorns, berries and insects and grasses. To repay Adams for his kindness and largess, the redskins cut and dried grass from the meadows to make winter hay for his stock and then helped him tan deerskins and make suits of buckskins, to replace the woolen miner's clothing which was wearing out. (Although Grizzly Adams would live in San Francisco and New York, he never returned to civilized clothing during the rest of his life.) He still clung to his long woolen underwear—or, rather, it clung to him—but over it went winter gear of buck-skin pants, coat and moccasins, an untanned deerskin cap lined with rabbit fur for warmth and trimmed with a fox's tail. This ensemble became his distinctive costume forever-more.

At last, the morning light which dappled the scabby bark of the great ponderosas no longer carried any warmth. Winter's heavy hand lay upon the Range of Light. As their ancestors had done for hundreds of years before them, the Indians moved downriver with the change in season and, before the first snow fell, Adams was entirely alone on the Stanislaus. Yet the next weeks were among the happiest he ever spent. He was snug and warm in his shelter; he never let his fire die out. There was plenty of game; he was never hungry. Besides meat, the animals he killed provided him with a surfeit of furs and skins for clothing so he stored them, along with tallow and oil, to trade or sell for cash in the settlements after spring should climb into the mountains again. He also trapped a number of live animals that winter —deer, wolves, beaver, rabbits, mink and four grizzlies which (in only *one* of his two major reminiscences) he said he trained and tamed in order to exhibit them for profit.

Every day was an adventure but winter held no hardship for Adams. The ice-cold water was the purest and most refreshing he had ever tasted. He kept himself busy during the deep snows when he did not choose to hunt by trying out new kinds of food such as his Indian friends used. He pounded grass seeds into meal or flour; he roasted acorns to make a passable kind of coffee. From the bruises in the bark of the big-coned sugar pines he harvested the sweet gum or sap called pine sugar. His only neighbors were animals and all of them gave him a wide berth except the grizzlies. They feared nothing, man included. But neither did they seek combat and Adams was happy to live in a state of truce with them.

29

Winter died and spring brought the grass forth in the mountain meadows and filled the brooks and streams to overflowing. Now Adams began to think of hunting the giant grizzlies in earnest. He wished to test his courage and skill against an animal the scientists called *Ursus ferox* and *Ursus horribilis*, the fierce and horrible bear, the one animal more dangerous than the African lion, the Cape buffalo, or even the Indian tiger which had maimed him long before.

In the spring of 1853 he dropped down to Mariposa with one of his bears, to wrestle him in public. Not only did he win fame, or notoriety, locally, but he also netted $800 for his rough-and-tumble prowess at grappling with *ursus*. Two men, McSheer and Robinson, asked him to deliver his other three live bears to them. They planned to take them all to South America to exhibit them there, stage bear-pit fights, and split the profits, 50-50, with Adams.* Though teams were scarce and roads ranged from bad to impassable, he was able to hire teamsters and rigs at a ranch, perhaps Howard's near Hornitos, and delivered the animals to Stockton in good shape. He also disposed of his winter's take of hides and pelts but even the finest plews did not raise his profit to $300, which barely covered the expenses of getting the bears to the river port. Adams was speedily returned to his proper role, that of pauper, again.

But at William J. Howard's ranch, near the Merced River, Adams ran into a young Texan named Saxon.** He was part-Indian, a proficient woodsman and a pretty fair shot. Adams took a liking to the younger man with the coarse black hair, high cheekbones and dark complexion of an Indian. He told

---

* This version makes more sense than the other one Adams told, in which a visitor to his camp, wishing to secure wild bears for exhibition on the East Coast, turned out to be his own brother, William! Since Adams had no brother named William—although he himself, for reasons known only to him, used the name William when he first went to San Francisco—this tale has to be from somewhere west of Apocrypha.

** According to his 1856 story, told to Hittell, his friend was William Syke-sey; his 1860 account has the man's name as Saxon, and nickname Saxey.

Grizzly that he had been in the Pacific Northwest and the woods there were even wilder than California's. He told such interesting stories of his adventures with black and white wolves, and grizzlies, in that desolate region, a "paradise of a wilderness," that Adams decided, on the spot, to make that his destination rather than go to the High Sierra. Saxon agreed to join him and share, alike, in the proceeds of their hunts. Adams traded his oxen to William J. Howard for two mules and, with the Texan, broke his camp between the Tuolumne and Stanislaus and made his way to Strawberry Ranch, some ten miles east. There, Grizzly hired two more hands for his expedition. They were young Indian boys * whose real names he disregarded, probably because he could not pronounce the tongue-twisting language of the Diggers. He called them after the tribe, or area, from which they came —Tuolumne and Stanislaus. Each of the four men, dressed in buckskins, carried a rifle—"loaded for b'ar"—on his back and a pistol and skinning knife on his belt. Packed on the mules was the bedding, the flour, sugar, salt and other provisions necessary for a successful journey of a thousand miles and return. Apparently Adams tried to make gear for the pack mules of the harness he had used on his oxen. He soon found that it would not work so he called a halt and made harness of green elkskin. Again they set forth but again they had to stop. The rawhide was cutting the mules' skin and Grizzly had to cover it with soft, tanned deerskin.

On a delightful, sun-washed morning in April or May 1853, the quartet set out from Strawberry Ranch on their northward course. Adams kept to the shoulders of the mountains, leaving the snowy crests to his right. It would have been much easier going down in the Sacramento Valley but

---

* Twenty-year-olds in his 1856 memory, the boys were 14-15 years old in his New York reminiscence of four years later. In the latter account Adams stated that he hired them during the winter to help him capture wild animals and guard his goods when he had to be away from his camp, rather than as companions for his Rocky Mountain trip.

he preferred to make his northing at a higher altitude. He was willing to trade the comfort of level valley travel for the game he was able to take so easily at the more alpine elevation. In just two weeks of up-and-down travel across the cañons and arroyos of the Sierra slopes, the four arrived in the Klamath area. Near Klamath Lake, Adams narrowly missed killing or capturing the rarest, most bizarre animal he had ever seen. The beast, which looked like a hedgehog with the head and feet of a bear, escaped.

North of Klamath Lake, Adams led his men through a howling wilderness between the Cascade Mountains and the Blue Mountains of Oregon. Mount Jefferson and Mount Hood soon loomed to the left, kept even with them, and were left behind. Very fatigued, the four men finally met the Columbia River after four weeks of the hardest sort of trekking. They crossed the Snake, or (Meriwether) Lewis's River, and headed for the country lying to the northeast. At last they came to a valley whose looks Adams liked. Like Brigham Young, he said "This is the place," and his men dropped their loads, stretched out on the ground and relaxed. Adams had found a valley in the hills with plenty of water. It was not too close to, nor too far from, the nearest Indian village. The old mountaineer wanted a good ten miles between him and the redmen.

Either here, or even before he set up camp, Adams began his efforts to lasso young bears for eventual sale. Although he had plenty of help now, he still preferred to hunt alone. He explained his reasoning, much later, for Phineas T. Barnum: "The safety of Number One [i.e., himself] is just about as much as I find I have leisure to look after. A faltering of the heart, a quivering of the finger, a vibration of the rifle, a shot in a non-vital part of the animal instead of the heart, so as to enrage and not disable her—all these are possible things at any time and when they occur, heaven help Number Two, for Number One will have his hands full and the grizzly is

ıot particular as to whether she kills one or a dozen men
'or dinner when she goes marketing in such a state of excitement!"

In this easternmost corner of wild Washington Territory,
Adams found an abundance of curly-haired brown bears,
which he took to be relatives of California's grizzlies although
they did not attain the great size of their presumed kin—up
to a ton—nor were they as savage. Not far from camp, in a
thick stand of chaparral, Grizzly Adams discovered a bear's
den at the end of a well-worn trail. The hunter determined
to waylay and shoot the mother bear in order to seize and
tame her two young cubs. He hid himself just off the trail
one morning when the animals were returning from the valley. As the adult bear came into view, Adams drew a bead
on her and fired. The half-ounce ball sped true and the
animal fell with the bullet in her chest. But, to Adams's surprise, the bear quickly recovered and charged him. He hardly
had time to drop his rifle, pick up the other, and shoot from
the hip. His quick shot went through the beast's open mouth
and into the brain.

Ascertaining that the mother was down this time for keeps,
Grizzly laid his rifle aside and caught up his reata. He tried
to lasso the two cubs, like a California vaquero. But the
bumbling youngsters proved to be far less clumsy than they
looked and easily evaded the hunter's loop by zigzagging in
and out of thickets of brush. When Adams was winded from
his shanks'-mare pursuit of them, the little cubs turned on
him and, although they were only a year old or so, shortly
persuaded him with their sharp claws and teeth to climb a
tree. Later on, it made the great grizzly hunter laugh to think
back to the day he was treed by a pair of infantile bruins.
But it was annoying at the time. The bears tried to climb up
after him and he had to pound on their paws to discourage
them. Luckily for Adams, they had not yet learned the patience of their elders and were not up to waiting him out

at the base of the tree. They wandered off in a half hour and Adams was able to descend and return to camp.

Things were starting off on the wrong foot for the bear catcher. But Adams was as stubborn as his pack mules and he came up with a new plan. Knowing the cubs would not leave their mother's body for some days, he mounted a mule and rode down to the Indian village, or *rancheria* as he called it from California habit. He took with him his two Digger boys to act as interpreters, and a present of jerked venison for Chief Kennasket. This he turned over to the chief, who seemed suspicious of whites but who appreciated the gift. Kennasket agreed to lend Adams three horses—"lasso horses" —to use in chasing the cubs onto the plains where they would find no cover in which they could hide. Ordinary horses would not do, and Adams was particular about his choices. ("A horse must be specially trained to the use of a rider who is a lassoist, and mules are out of the question," Adams later explained.) In exchange, Adams promised the chief a sack of dried meat each day for each horse borrowed. The Indian sent one of his braves, whom Adams nicknamed Pompey, to make sure that the white stranger returned the mounts.

The next morning, Adams found the cubs near the dead bear and, with two of his men, charged down on them like a dragoon captain, hoping to drive them down the trail to the open country. But once again the cubs dodged into the bushes and he was forced to call a halt to the pursuit which, even with horses, was impossible.

On the third morning there was no sign of the cubs but he knew that they would have to come to the one spring in the valley for water so, as soon as it was dark, he concealed himself, alone, in ambush near the water hole. Try as he might, however, he could not stay awake and his vigil was broken by light dozing which turned into a deep sleep as he lay in the heavy sword grass. It must have been midnight when he was awakened by a noise. In the moonlight he could see that it was the cubs passing. But, they were on their way back to the tangle of mountain buckbrush! Once again they had outwitted him. Adams sprang after them but he knew, all too well, that pursuit was hopeless and they vanished easily into the dark shadows.

Unwilling to return to camp empty-handed, the hunter continued to crouch in the grass near the spring. He had studied the tracks in the mud and saw that it was visited by thirsty cougars or mountain lions, wolves, deer and antelope as well as slippery cubs. First came a pack of wolves. They drank silently but then uttered a horrible toast in the form of bloodcurdling howls. Adams put them to flight with a rifle ball directed toward their gleaming eyes. The identity of the next visitor was betrayed by its heavy tread. From its footsteps, Adams knew it was a bear. He yelled to attract its attention and the animal, a large black bear, reared up on its hind legs. With such a target, Adams could hardly miss and for several days thereafter the men enjoyed bear steaks in camp.

The next night, Adams and all of his men waited at the spring. They let antelope, deer and wolves come and go unmolested and the sky was a light gray with streaks of light in it before they heard the playful yelps of the cubs. He let them drink, wallow and tumble and wrestle on the grass for a few minutes. Then he gave a shrill whistle and all four men kicked their mounts in the ribs with their heels and galloped down on the animals. The cubs separated and Adams chased one while his men charged after the other. After a run of a mile, the hunter got his lariat over the cub's head but the animal pawed it off. This act was repeated again and again. On the eighth cast of his rope, and after a four-mile chase, Adams was finally able to drop the noose neatly over the cub's head. He jerked his horse to a stop, snubbing the bear. Leaping off his horse, he examined his catch and found that it was a young female. While his horse backed skillfully to keep the lariat taut, Adams muzzled the cub's jaws with a short piece of rope and, with rawhide thongs, tied her fore feet. Tying the rear feet was a real struggle as the animal regained her strength, but eventually he had the she-cub trussed up as neatly as a Christmas package.

Adams then returned to see how his companions were faring. He found that they had chased their quarry, a male, into such a thick stand of brush that it had become entangled and helpless. They had dismounted, seized him and bound him securely. In fact, Adams had never seen an animal so wound up in rope. He looked like a mummy. He had bitten and scratched them so savagely they wished to make sure he had no opportunity of repeating the process. Slinging their captive over their shoulders from a long pole, they bore him in triumph to the spring where Adams was resting. They did not notice Adams's cub so, in great glee, they proceeded to show off their trophy, assuming that he had failed in his quest. Their triumph was cut short when the Yankee quietly asked to see where they had caught the animal. When he was shown the thicket, he remarked that it was certainly an easier place than his cub's refuge on the open prairie. Next, he compared his hands and arms, unmarked, with their lacerated hands. "Look at your hands," he said. "Mine are not scratched in that way. There is no blood there." He told them of his success and could not help boasting (modesty, after all, was not one of Grizzly's vices) a little, to get even with them for their eagerness to show him up. "She is the prettiest little animal in all the country." Both Saxey and Tuolumne thought that he was joking but rather than going back for the cubs, Adams just looked them straight in the eye and bellowed, "Have you ever known the Old Hunter to lie?" "No," answered the Texan and the Digger, squirming uncomfortably under the glare which cowed even grizzlies. Then, and only then, did he show them the cub he had just caught.

His new problem was how to get the live trophies back to

camp. Saxey, or Sykesey, suggested binding the cubs up and hauling them on horseback. Tuolumne preferred fastening them in a drag of grass and towing them along behind the horse. It is not entirely clear just what was Adams's decision, since he changed his story so frequently. In 1860, he said that he decided in favor of a drag but scorned the Indian's brush or grass idea. Instead, he led his men back to camp, selected a large elk hide and hitched his powerful mules to it. Returning to the trussed-up cubs, he gave them a bumpy ride to camp, travois-style. On the other hand, in his dictation to Thomas Hittell in 1856, Adams said that he had used a different method on each of the animals:

He placed a buckskin strap around the male cub's neck and attached a lariat to each side. With this, the men were able to lead him, once his fetters were removed, but he pranced and jumped so and they had to dodge the swipes of his claws so often that the men were worn out by the time they reached camp. (The cub was exhausted, too.) While his men rested, Adams doused the cub with cold water to refresh him, after chaining him to a tree, and tried to come up with a better method of retrieving the female, whom he now dubbed Lady Washington for the land of her birth. He thought he might make a sort of box or cage of dried hide, to pack her on horseback, but Pompey said that he would get a cart for the white hunter. When he returned with the vehicle, it was the strangest-looking contraption Adams had ever seen. It had two solid wheels, like a Mexican-California *carreta,* but nothing else save a tongue, axletree and, instead of a body, or bed, just a green stretched hide. The harness and traces were made of dried elk strips, rubbed until soft, fastened together with strings of elk hide. Instead of collars, the two horses pulled against two broad bands of hide and the tongue of the cart was held between the horses by thongs tied to their shoulder bands. When he asked Pompey what kept the cart from overrunning the horses on a downhill passage, the Indian answered that Indian carts were made to go forward only and that it was a bad horse which could not keep out of a cart's way.

To Adams's surprise, the cart worked. As the men approached the camp, they came upon a pack of wolves tearing at some carrion. The Indians shouted, in Spanish, *"Lobos!"* They turned to Adams and asked him to kill the hated animals. He fired and brought one of them down. To his amazement, the Indians skinned the animal. He had thought that wolf pelts were not worth the powder and ball expended in shooting the critter; now he learned that the Indians made leggings of the skins. The five hunters ended their day around a roaring fire, with a great feast of bear steaks, venison jerky and a nightcap from Adams's leather whiskey bottle. Since he knew his rifle would keep his party well supplied with food he did not worry but he was startled at the appetite of his new Indian friends. He later told a friend, "These Indians, whatever may be their failings in other respects, are terrible fellows with their jaws."

The old patriarch, Kennasket, was pleased that Adams carried out his contract to the letter, delivering him the meat as promised and returning the horses. He was not used to such honest dealings from white men. The chief offered Adams his pipe and they smoked together, after which they shook hands and Adams returned to his camp on a mule. He liked these Indians just as he liked California's Diggers and, for that matter, all Indians. Adams, more than ever, felt that the blame for all the Indian troubles of the West lay with the whites, not with the redmen who were his friends.

To replenish his camp's provisions, devoured by his visitors the night before, Adams led his men out on the grassy plain the next day to hunt antelope, the fastest, keenest-scented and sharpest-eyed animal in the West. But the white hunter knew of its fatal weakness, if his companions did not. Because he knew that each antelope had more curiosity than a platoon of cats, Adams ordered his men to surround the herd which he had spied on the prairie, then told Pompey to raise and wave a red handkerchief. This he did. The herd's lookout spotted it, swiveled toward it and snorted a signal. The whole herd then wheeled around to stare at the fluttering bandanna. As they huddled together, all facing Pompey, Adams, with Saxey and Tuolumne, crept up close to them through the rank grass. When he was sixty yards away, Adams stood up and fired. His two companions followed suit and the Indians filled the air with arrows. Adams reloaded hurriedly, fired again, dropped his rifle and charged into the center of the herd with his pistol in his right hand and his bowie knife in his left. Soon there was a lunging, dusty scrimmage of men and animals and when a buck finally broke the confused circle and led the herd away, the hunters had eleven animals to butcher for their larder.

The Indians grinned their pleasure and amazement at Adams and pronounced him "muchee goodee killee muck-a-muck," which was to say "a great hunter." He shrugged off their praise, lying politely that what he had done was a mere nothing to any white hunter. But they insisted that he was a real *hyas tyee,* or great chief.

The men settled down to the chore of packing the meat to camp. Normally, Adams would have thrown the innards away, as unsuitable for eating, but they were now taken to camp along with the good meat in order to feed the bears. Adams never could resist playing practical jokes. (Undoubtedly, he lost more than one friend, temporarily or permanently, as a result.) He told the Indians that he would let them have any antelope which they could carry all the way into camp, three miles away. Three warriors tried but all failed, dropping their loads from exhaustion. But Adams was only teasing them. He intended giving them the meat all along and he loaned them a mule to carry it. Again, he could not resist giving Tuolumne a good scare when he found him stretched out, asleep, in the grass. Since he was supposed to be guarding the meat, Adams decided it was proper to teach him a lesson. He took a bearskin, used for a saddle blanket on one of the mules, wrapped himself in it, and crawled up through the grass, growling as he neared the sleeping Indian. Tuolumne stiffened in alarm, came to, and leaped to his feet as if he were on a steel spring. When he stooped to pick up his rifle, Adams let out a louder and more menacing growl and the California brave abandoned gun, meat and all, and ran like the wind. Adams followed him, growling and snorting, until the lad disappeared. Then the hunter picked up his rifle and, collecting his mules, rode leisurely into camp.

There he found Tuolumne regaling everyone with a tale of being pursued by a ferocious and enormous bear. Adams, to prolong his joke, pretended to believe him and when they rolled up in their blankets for the night, warned Tuolumne to keep a sharp lookout. "That bear," said the hunter, "has got a smell of your meat and he will be sure to call on you before morning." He continued to tease him until the youth became very alarmed, then Adams relented. He told him exactly what had happened and lectured him on cowardice. But Tuolumne would not believe it. What he saw with his own eyes he would believe. Adams sighed, rolled over, and went to sleep.

CHAPTER III

URSUS HORRIBILIS

ⓞN his hunting forays, Adams sometimes carried the cubs in a hamper on the backs of the mules but usually he left them tethered in camp. They were chained to pine trees by leather straps around their necks. The Yankee hunter customarily hunted from dawn to dusk but he rested, every day, at noon. During these midday breaks he trained the cubs. He found Lady Washington to be "ugly" not in appearance, but in temper. This pleased the cranky hermit. He explained, "I fell in love with the cub because she *was* so ill-natured. I felt a species of delight in subduing, little by little, a will so resolute and a temper so obstinate. I had my reward, besides, in my confidence of success."

Convinced now that lassoing was no way in which to capture animals alive, for a menagerie, the huntsman set about building three box traps to place in areas frequented by all kinds of beasts. Soon the axes, saws and chisels he had brought from the Stanislaus were ringing and flashing in the Washington sunlight. Each cage was to be ten feet long, five feet wide, and five feet high. Each would require seventy pieces of timber. Since he had no nails, Adams had to hew out a large number of wooden pins to take their place. He fastened the strong boxlike structures to trees and to posts in order to give them even greater strength and rigidity. The heavy trapdoors were tripped by a piece of bait attached, by rope, to a system of levers and forked sticks.

Grizzly believed in getting to work early so, for two weeks or more, he rousted his men out of their blankets an hour before sunrise to haul timber with the mules or to split out puncheons for floors, walls and doors of the traps. Everything went well until the tough-grained logs rebelled at the dulling edges of the axes and wedges which Adams employed so skillfully for splitting them. But he knew a trick or two. Remembering his old days in the New England forests, he copied a method used there by the Down Easters. He bored holes in the logs with his auger, loaded them with gunpowder and blasted the logs into pieces which he and his men could shape with their ax work.

The result of a full fortnight's labor was a set of traps so strong that Adams never feared that any animal might escape. He was later proved wrong when a thousand-pound grizzly, with the temper of ten, began dismantling the pen by shaking and biting it to pieces. When Adams came upon it, the beast had almost gnawed his way to freedom right through the timbers and, though he did not like to kill a caged and temporarily helpless animal, he had to shoot the grizzly. When he and his men tried to drag the carcass from the half-wrecked cage, they found they could not budge the monster and Adams had to hitch the mules to haul out the remains of *Ursus horribilis.*

Adams also met up with the curious beasts he called "hyena black bears." He killed a female of the species in order to capture her tiny, toothless, cubs and found that he had to place four rifle balls in vital organs before she would give up the ghost. When she finally collapsed, he bundled the squalling and bawling creatures into the saddlebags which he had made on the model of those he had used back in Massachusetts. They differed from the traditional New England variety only in that they were square and had lids which could be closed. The cubs made such a din in their close quarters that their father came crashing through the brush to succor them. Adams, hurriedly reloading his piece, sicked his dog on the bruin. The fearless hound "took" the bear, dancing about just out of reach of its snapping muzzle and distracting the beast with his barking and movement until Adams could snap a shot which dropped the irate parent. Back at camp, Adams gave the infants flour and water, sweetened with sugar. They throve on it.

The hard work of building the big traps made the men hungry, always, and Adams, who never killed unless he needed meat or skins, was kept busier than ever with his rifle. Some of the venison went to the men; some, as bait, to the traps. He had a narrow escape at this time when trying to procure some bear steaks for his hungry carpenters. Hunting with Saxey one day, Adams let him fire first at a hyena bear. The rifle ball hit its target but seemed only to madden the animal. Then Adams fired. Again the bullet's trajectory carried it to the mark but the bear, after reeling and staggering a little, regained its balance and came after the Wild Yankee, open-jawed. Adams coolly let it rush to within a few feet of him, then the fearless mountainer fired his pistol right into its muzzle. The heavy ball pierced the brute's nose and carried into its brain. It fell over backward, dead, but its rush had carried it almost on top of the hunter. Only when the shaggy beast lay stiff did Adams relax his grip on the bowie knife he held tightly in his left hand, which had been his last hope.

Only a few days after this narrow squeak, it was a grizzly's turn to try Adam's courage. That day, the attention of all the men was attracted by the clatter of rocks and the breaking of branches on a steep hill near the traps. They saw a big female grizzly coming down the hill, backward. She looked silly but the men held their laughter because she looked ornery, too. Adams whispered to Saxey to hand him his rifle and cautioned the Texas half-breed to back him up and to fire if his own ball did not stop the animal. When the she-bear reached the base of the hill where the men were, Adams blazed away. The light was failing and the crack shot's aim was bad. He missed the brute entirely. Before the smoke of his exploded black powder had barely been torn away by the breeze, Adams's ears were deafened. Saxey's rifle went off right beside his head. Adams, who turned to see his comrade, wheeled to view the bear again; if Number Two's hurried shot had missed, they were in a bad situation. The Texan *had* missed. He panicked and fled as fast as he could pick up and lay down his moccasins. Left to face the grizzly alone, Adams whirled, crouched with braced legs and prepared to sell his life dearly with the bowie knife in his hand. To his amazement, the huge bulk of the bear hurtled right past him, almost brushing him. The grizzly had not seen him in the deepening dusk but was intent on killing Saxey.

The Texan was putting plenty of Washington Territory between the grizzly and himself when suddenly he fell over a downed tree and it looked to all of the men as if their comrade was a goner. But, dropping his knife, Adams had feverishly reloaded. The beast tumbled over the fallen log and crashed almost atop Saxey, who was trying desperately to scramble away. Adams took aim. He recalled the scene, years later: "The bear rose on her legs, opened her forepaws to embrace him in a mortal hug, gave a terrific roar that showed a frightful head of teeth and glared on him like a fiend dressed in fur." Just at the critical moment, the hunter's rifle cracked and the grizzly dropped, dead.

Adams ran up to Saxey, but not to inquire into his health. The Texan, unhurt but terrified, stammered something about his gun going off prematurely, by accident. He then mumbled something about his thinking it best to try to save his skin, in the circumstances. Adams cut him short with a glare and, his voice dripping with sarcasm and disgust, read him the riot act, accusing the Texan of performing exactly according to his cowardly nature. Reminding him that a brave man would have faced the danger, he said, "It is the character of a coward to run, though he drag after him not only disgrace but danger, too."

When Adams was done with his verbal thrashing of his companion, it was pitch-dark. Incredibly, Saxey—who should have known enough to keep his mouth shut—ventured to Grizzly that he did not think he would be of any help to him if they met a bear by night. Adams's temper flared up again. "It's not likely that a man will stand fast at night who will run in the day." But he added with mock compassion, "Do not be alarmed. You have the choice of staying here—alone." The idea of being left by himself all night in bear country horrified the shaken Texan and he trotted meekly to camp at Adams's heels, the mountaineer not deigning even to look back for him, much less speak to him.

The truth of the old saw about things coming in threes was proved to Adams on the last day of trap building. Hunting fresh meat for bait in the morning, he came upon a band of a half-dozen elk. The leader was a big buck with a fine rack of antlers and it was this individual which Adams chose to shoot. Because he could get no closer without spooking the wapiti, Adams had to fire at a range of seventy-five yards. The buck fell, however, so he laid his rifle in the grass and advanced on the animal with his skinning knife in hand. He always cut the throat of a downed animal, just to be on the safe side, even in the case of deer, elk and other nondangerous animals. He knelt beside the wapiti, ready to cut with the blade when suddenly the animal, only stunned, came to its senses. The elk sprang erect and shot out its forelegs like two battering rams. The sharp hooves dug into Adams's neck and shoulder and his bowie knife was sent flying from his paralyzed hand. With his other hand, he drew his Colt from its holster and emptied it, point-blank, into the body of the

45

rampant elk. These shots did not kill the maddened animal but one of the slugs hit it at the base of the ear and stunned it again, giving Adams time to grasp his knife and plunge it into the elk's heart.

That day, Adams proved to his awestruck companions just how tough a critter he was. While his men marveled, he worked the rest of the day in the hot sun despite his bruised and bloody shoulders and, that evening, he helped pack the elk meat to camp. At dinner, he enjoyed a fine roast, courtesy of the animal which had almost killed him a few hours before. He remarked, to no one in particular, that it was as good as porterhouse steak. Tuolumne pricked up his ears. The euphony of the term possibly intrigued the inquisitive Digger. In any case, he asked Adams what was "porterhouse-steak." As the hunter explained about this choice cut of beef, the Indian repeated and repeated the words to commit them to memory. For the rest of their acquaintance, Tuolumne used the term porterhouse steak when he wished to signify to Adams that he found something to be excellent, whether it was meat or not.

The work on his "trap huts," as he called them, was soon finished and Adams, none the worse from his bloody encounter, got his men to gather old wood and grass and to smoke the traps well in order to give them an old look and smell and to drive away the human odor which would cause suspicious grizzlies to give them a wide berth. Before baiting the traps, he mounted a mule and dragged a quarter of elk meat on the end of a lariat in a great circle around each trap. Now, all the hunters had to do was to wait.

While they waited, Adams began the training of the two black bear cubs, George Washington and Buchanan, the latter named not for the President but in honor of an old hunter of the area whom Grizzly met. ("He fancied that it would be something agreeable to stand godfather to the cub, and I yielded to his wish," said the Yankee.) The black bear cubs were tame already and roamed about camp like pet dogs when they were not gamboling together in mock wrestling matches. The two even slept with Adams, under his blanket, by the fire. From time to time, of nights, he had to box their ears for being too squirmy. The more dangerous grizzly cubs had to be kept chained all the time. Although Adams went out of his crusty way to be kind to them, and particularly to Lady Washington, they repaid him by jumping and snapping at him whenever he came too close. Finally, his patience was exhausted. He decided he would have to give the female cub a good whipping. He went to a nearby ravine, selected and cut a stout stick and began to thrash her with it. This drubbing made her Ladyship furious, more from rage than hurt. She jumped about, growled and lunged at him. Adams hated to beat her, for she was his favorite, but it seemed to be the only thing to do to tame her. Sure enough, after this severe spanking, she became more docile and let him pat her hairy hide. Day by day, she became calmer. For her good conduct, Adams gave her a greater length of chain so that she would have more freedom to roam. When he fed her, from then on, she not only ate more heartily but with apparent gratitude, or so it appeared to her tamer. The next step in her training was for him to remove the chain entirely and to lead her about camp by a lariat tied to her collar. A rap on her back with a stick, now and then, took away her stubbornness.

Lady Washington's brother, Jackson, was even harder to train. When Adams tried to lead him about, he would sit on his rump, refuse to move and place his paw on the chain, growling in a menacing manner. The hunter tried a different technique in schooling Jackson from that used on his sister. Instead of spanking him with a stick, Adams tied one end of his reata to the bear's collar and the other to his saddle horn. He then giddaped his mule into a run and the big-eared mount would tow the protesting bear across the meadow and through patches of stinging stiff-limbed brush. The surly grizzly made the mistake of snapping at the heels of the mule and, for his pains, got the jolt of his life. The mule, an expert in this sort of work, delivered him a kick which sent him sprawling. Bruised but wiser, the bruin began to follow, sulkily, wherever Adams chose to lead him. After some minutes of this, Adams jumped off his mule and began to lead the bear on a *paseo* with the lariat. Jackson tried to balk by sitting down but Grizzly just administered a few whacks with his club and the bear regained his feet, grumbling but moving on. By the end of that one day of schooling, Adams was able to pat him on the head and to scratch his neck. The hunter had proved, at least partially, his belief that if grizzlies were taken young enough and treated well but firmly enough, they could become as good-humored and as devoted companions as dogs.

Inspecting the traps one day, Adams found that one of them had been visited but not sprung. His keen eyes and sense of woodcraft told him that the visitor had been a wolf and he quickly found out why old *lobo* had gotten away scot-free; the trap's catch had been set so that the bait would not spring it. Adams easily remedied that and told Tuolumne that he would have the wolf for keeps, and soon. "How do you know that?" the California Indian asked him. "It's the nature of the beast to return," answered Adams.

When the heat of that day was over, the two men took a ride into a new region where they happened upon a pack of black wolves. Their guns brought down two of them and a third, wounded, hopped away. Adams, confident—reckless —as usual, put aside his rifle and dropped down a bank to chase the hobbling *lobo* with his knife. He caught up, seized the animal expertly by the tail and flipped it over onto the ground. But, once again, Adams's overconfidence betrayed and hurt him—hurt him more painfully this time than had the hooves of the angry elk. Before the hunter could stab it, the wolf twisted its muzzle upright and sank its fangs into Adams's forearm. The pain was so severe in his right arm that he saw the bowie knife drop from his stiffening fingers. For a moment, Adams could do nothing but try to protect his throat. But when the dizzying wave of pain lessened for a moment, he reached across his body with his left hand, yanked the Colt out of its holster in a desperate cross draw, and shot the wolf in the heart.

Tuolumne (and, later, Saxey) thought the wound would lay Adams up for a week, at least. But they did not count on the strength of the white hunter or his faith in what he called his water cure. For medicine in the wilds, Adams used nothing but pure water. He had Tuolumne soak his handkerchief in cold water and wrap it tightly around the wound like a wet bandage. Then he sent him on to camp with the carcasses of the three wolves while he followed more slowly behind, alone. "What will you do with your lame arm if you are attacked?" his Indian friend asked him. "There's nothing to fear," was Adams's nonchalant answer.

To his amazement, shortly after the Indian left, a coyote, probably attracted by the smell of blood, trotted up and impudently barked and snarled at the great hunter. It was infuriating to Adams to see the cur apparently getting up courage to nip at him. His paining arm contributing to his annoyance, Adams drew his revolver and shot the miserable animal and kicked its body off the trail. But now it was dark and he finally had to admit something which, as a mountain man, hurt him even more than his arm. He was lost.

Adams did not know in which direction to strike so, weak from loss of blood, he just sat down. He would climb a tree, he thought, and look for the glare of his friends' campfire, which could not be too far away. But suddenly he heard a scream like that of a woman, nearby. Adams was too good a mountain man to be fooled by that. He knew it was the cry of a cougar, or puma. He also knew that the mountain lion

49

was a coward, generally, but that one attacking from ambush in the dark on a bloody trail could be deadly. He strained to pierce the darkness, wishing that he had another pair of eyes. As Adams later told his newspaperman friend, Thomas H. Hittell, "Under ordinary circumstances, a brave man with a pistol and knife can protect himself against any panther but with a lame arm, and weak from hunger and fatigue, I might have been badly injured, perhaps killed."

When the beast screamed again, Adams tightened his grip on his rifle, sure now that the animal was looking for a good place from which to spring upon him in the dark. But when the big cat shrieked for a third time, it was farther away and to windward, which meant that Adams's scent, and the smell of his bloody wounds, had not carried to it. The hunter finally found a pine which he could climb with only one useful arm and from a limb he saw the reflection of a fire being freshened. Apparently his men were tending it to guide him home. Cheered, he descended from his perch and hurried over rough hills and down bushy ravines. By the time he was near camp, however, he was completely exhausted and almost asleep. Finally, he could go no farther. But Old Adams could still bellow. He let out a series of yells which rang through the wilderness. His men heard his halloing and rushed to help him. As they carried him to the fire, he could only croak, "Give me some water! Give me some food!"

Saxey and the others gave him water to drink and some roast venison to eat and soon Adams could feel his strength returning. It was apparently hunger and thirst more than fatigue and loss of blood which had sent him to his knees, exhausted. Before he turned to his blankets, he had Tuolumne pour a stream of cold water directly onto the wounds in his forearm. Then he had him replace the bandage, wrapping the entire arm from fingers to shoulder. Adams then turned in for the night, having more than earned a good rest.

CHAPTER IV

WHITE HUNTER

EVEN as indestructible a man as John Adams had to have some rest after the mauling he had taken from the wolf, so he lay about camp for a day or two. He disdained shelter, except a few boughs overhead when it rained, preferring just to lay his blankets out on the ground with a pillow made of a bag of dried grass. Whereas his friends crowded up close to the fire, their feet practically toasting in the coals, cautious Old Adams always had his blanket roll spread in the shadows so that he could see well into the firelit area but so that any intruders could not easily see him. Adams was always ready for an attack. For a day or so after the wolf bit him, the morning star caught Adams still in his bed, and sunrise found him still in camp rather than out on a hunt. But two days of leisure, sleeping, eating and smoking wild (Indian) tobacco was enough for the battered but restless Adams. Since he no longer hated everybody, as had been the case when he first turned his back on civilization in California, and he was bored with camp, he decided that it was a good time to visit his Indian neighbors.

Taking Tuolumne with him, he proceeded with the mules to Chief Kennasket's village of Nez Percés or Pend d'Oreilles. (Adams was never sure to which of the two tribes his neighbors belonged.) Realizing that Indians always loved pomp and circumstance, he stole a leaf from Meriwether Lewis's book and sent Tuolumne ahead, ceremoniously bearing a white flag. Kennasket was delighted with this herald and sent a message back with "Gray Beard's" equerry that he was always welcome at the lodge of his friend. Adams then drove the mules, loaded with meat, grandly up to the tepees where the squaws took care of it, chattering about his grand entrance—one that would not soon be forgotten in that village.

Kennasket offered to lend him his horses again, whereupon the Old Hunter, alias Gray Beard, thanked him and gesturing to the meat, said that he always kept his promises. After exchanging presents for a good half hour, Indian-fashion, Adams was ready to go but the chief motioned for him to stay. He wanted to give his white friend a present, something which he should keep as long as he lived, in memory of Great Chief Kennasket. Adams, having no idea what the marvelous present might be, replied that not only would he value it highly, he would hold it sacred. The hunter's mind rambled over an imaginary display of presents. Could it be a fine calumet or peace pipe? Or perhaps a necklace of bear claws or a belt of wampum? To his surprise and disappointment, the chief returned bearing a little black puppy. While Tuolumne snickered, Adams managed, somehow, to look very interested and pleased, kneeling on the ground and cradling the little mutt against his chest as if it were an infant. Until the lodges were lost from sight, Adams did not dare to stop oohing and aahing over the bewildered puppy, for fear of offending Kennasket. Once back in camp, however, he left it to its own devices.

While Adams was ill, his men had kept busy tanning skins of animals they had killed. They used the age-old Indian method, rubbing the pelts with brains, although sometimes they added salt and alum and usually smoked them as a last step, using a convenient natural chimney in the shape of a hollow tree. The daily hunting and trapping of the California party in this happiest of hunting grounds paid off handsomely. They had bales of hides and such a store of oil and tallow that Adams and his companions began to feel rich. Adams admitted that during that summer's camp he had seen, in his mind's eye, future dollars leaking from the heaps of hides in the hut, which was fast becoming a rude warehouse.

When Adams was well again, it was time to check the traps. The day after being presented with the puppy by the Indians, Adams took Tuolumne to make the rounds of the hut traps. En route they came upon a band of antelope and gave chase on their mules. It was no contest. The stiff-legged mules could no more catch the swift antelope than they could capture Halley's comet. Adams had expected as much but the ridiculousness of the unequal race gave him and his Indian friend a good laugh.

In the first trap, just as he expected, he found a savage she-wolf and two whelps. She rushed madly within the confines of the cage to show her fangs to the men who peered into the crude box through a crack. To calm her down, Adams made a loop in a rope and lowered it through a hole in the top of the trap while Tuolumne engaged her attention by poking sticks through the cracks in the side walls. As she bit at one, Adams deftly looped the noose over her ears, pulled it tight around her neck and soon had a collar and lariat leash on her. The pups were so attached to their mother that, although they dashed into the screening brush as soon as Grizzly raised the trapdoor, they soon reappeared to tag along behind their snarling mama, in the tow of the men. Tuolumne was made nervous by the little wolves nipping and yapping at his heels but he soon began to tease them, until they were in such a frenzy that Adams had to stop him.

Upon their arrival at camp, Adams was greeted not only as a mighty hunter but also as a great prophet for his prediction that the *lobos*, without doubt, would return to the trap. It was not prophecy, just common sense and woodcraft, snorted Adams cantankerously as he tied his catch to several trees.

During the usual campfire conversation that night, Saxey asked how Adams had got the rope around the neck of the wolf trapped in the box trap. Gray Beard explained, whereupon Saxey said, "I never would have thought of such a plan." Adams's reply to this was an important bit of advice for the Texan if he chose to take it. It was also true of Adams himself, a hundred times over. What he said was, "To be a good hunter you must be a thousand things besides a good shot."

One morning, even earlier than Adams's usual hour for getting up, some sixth sense told him, as he lay in his blankets half asleep, to jump up and grab his weapon. He leaped to his feet, blinking sleep from his eyes, threw his rifle to his shoulder and made ready to repel an Indian attack. It was a visit of Indians, to be sure, but they were three startled braves from Chief Kennasket's village. Adams found himself looking over his sights at his hunting friend, Pompey. After they got over their fright, the three reported that they came to invite Adams to be a guest at a great feast which the chief was giving in two days. The hunter accepted, of course, but prevailed upon the trio to stay with him and help him hunt until it was time for the celebration, since he wanted to help Kennasket by bringing plenty of game. After breakfast, he formed up his men in two parties in order to cover a wider area. He led Pompey and another Indian in one direction, while Saxey took Tuolumne and the other brave on another course. Stanislaus, as usual, remained behind to guard the camp.

Hunting in the chaparral thickets, Adams soon killed a black bear and two deer while Saxey's party bagged several deer, one pronghorn, or antelope, and some smaller game. This was hardly a huge contribution to make to Kennasket's cookfires, so Adams gave his men orders to move out in the same hunting formation in the morning as they made their way toward the village. The men agreed to rendezvous at Kennasket's camp at evening. Stanislaus was interested in the celebration and Adams let him go, too. Saxey volunteered to guard the camp but Adams would not allow it, knowing that Kennasket expected both white hunters and if his aide failed to attend, the chief might be insulted. For once, he would leave his camp completely unguarded.

The next day, when Adams's party came upon a doe and two fawns feeding in a grassy meadow, the Indians with him asked if they could take the game with their bows and arrows rather than with his rifle. Adams readily agreed, since he was interested in seeing their hunting technique. The Indians dropped to the ground and crawled up to a point about three hundred yards from the grazing animals. Before continuing their stalking at closer quarters, they carefully and silently cut bunches of grass with their knives and wove them into caps which camouflaged their heads. In this grassy disguise, they again crept forward to within a hundred and fifty yards of the deer. In a third leg of their stalk, they writhed and wriggled through the grass like snakes and got within twenty to thirty yards without being detected. Then, in one motion, both sprang up, drew their bows and fired. The doe fell, with both arrows in its body, and the Indians pursued the fawns which fled into the brush. Adams was so pleased and impressed at the Indians' performance that he paced off the distances of their stalking and then congratulated them, calling them great hunters. They did not blush at this praise, as white men might have done, but although their eyes shone with pleasure, they did protest that their prowess was not so great and when Adams insisted, "You excel the White Hunter," they shook their heads and replied, "No, the White Hunter is a hunter of bears."

When he was within a few hundred yards of the Indian encampment, Adams sent one of the braves forward to announce his party in the good manners of the West. Shortly, one of the chief's squaws came up, bearing a wreath of wild flowers which she placed on the hunter's head. She then led him to the chief's tepee. In the lodge, Adams found Kennasket, his other wives, and his headmen. They all knelt as Adams entered and the chief made a little speech of welcome, telling all that the White Hunter was his good friend. Then Adams knelt and the Indians, making a circle around him, placed their hands on the crown of his head and repeated, in a singsong as they danced in a circle, the words of the chief: "Good is the White Hunter, who comes with much game from the east. No thief is he, but a friend and brother of the redman. He is welcome."

Next, it was Saxey's turn. And, even though Adams was pretty sure that he was partly of Indian blood, he knew the Texan would not know how to handle himself. So he decided to tease him again. The man's bewilderment at being crowned with flowers turned to suspicion when the Indians asked him to kneel. He turned to Adams, saying that he did not want to kneel; that he had never done such a thing for anyone in his life. Adams urged him to do so, saying, "You can surely kneel to say your prayers." As he saw the man's suspicious uneasiness turn to fear, the practical joker added, "Pluck up your courage and die like a man!" Much later, Adams told his newspaperman friend, Hittell, "For some reason, or other, I felt a kind of wicked pleasure in witnessing his imaginary terrors." Adams would not have been surprised to see Saxey keel over in a dead faint, but he managed to survive the confusing ordeal, even to dropping to his knees at the appointed time. But, thought Adams, as he watched the squaws dancing a sort of ring around the rosy, with Saxey in the middle, he looked more dead than alive.

When the ceremony was over, Saxey and Adams had a laugh together over the Texan's discomfiture and fright. Adams then led the way to the loaded mules and began to unpack them. He spread out a display of game which ranged

in size from birds, squirrels, rabbits and a badger to antelope, deer and bear. There were about forty animals in all.
Kennasket was pleased with the bounty and ordered some
of his braves to lead the mules to a meadow to graze. He
turned to Adams and said, "This night you shall sleep in my
lodge."

Grizzly politely but firmly declined, saying, "The White
Hunter never sleeps under cover, nor ever where women
sleep."

The chief laughed heartily at this and assured his guest
that his women would not harm anyone. But he respected
the hunter's strange medicine and let him suit himself. He
tried once more to be hospitable by pointing out some mats
hanging on his lodge's wall which, he said, were at his white
friend's service. But the stubborn Yankee again risked the
chief's displeasure, replying, "No, the White Hunter prefers
his blanket and the ground."

At this moment, dinner was announced by the squaws and
everyone sat down on the ground to tureens of a porridge
made of grass seeds and acorns, or of tule-root meal cooked in
water which had been heated by hot stones plopped into the
vessels. Side dishes included heaps of roasted meat served on
flat stones. Kennasket signaled to his guests to dig in, then led
the attack on the grub, himself. He cupped his kingly fingers
and, scooping them into the mush, brought a large gob neatly
up to his lips. Normally not too fastidious, Adams balked at
the public nature of the mush bowl, into which all present
were dipping and redipping their hands, so he addressed
himself to the joints of meat, assuring the chief that, person-
ally, he never ate mush.

To keep pace with the lip smacking of the piggish Indians,
Adams stuffed himself like an Alsatian goose, oohing and
aahing over the quality and flavor of the meat. When the
wreckage of the meal was cleared away at last, all knelt before
Kennasket who muttered a kind of grace and, after thus thank-

ing the Great Spirit for filling his belly, ventured that he would enjoy a repetition of the benefaction.

Instead of staying in the village, as invited, Adams borrowed a horse from Kennasket and rode to his own camp. He wanted to check on his wild wards, to see how they were holding up in his absence. He found that all was well in camp but, nevertheless, decided to sleep there, under his favorite tree. Long before dawn, the automatic alarm clock in his brain roused him. He saddled up and rode to the village, finding it as still as death. Giving in, once more, to his penchant for practical jokes, he spurred his horse into the compound, making as much noise as a troop of cavalry and shouting, "*Chawawi! Chawawi!*" the Indians' alarm signal. The whole tribe, perhaps 400 people in forty to fifty lodges, rushed out to do battle with the invader, only to find the whiskered old merrymaker laughing his sides sore.

Before breakfast, Adams looked over the chief's lodge, easily the handsomest structure in the village. It was a conical building in the center of the compound, built of long poles interlaced with woven branches and sticks. The whole dwelling, except for a smoke hole in the top, was plastered over with mud to keep the rain and cold winds out. The lodges of the braves and their families were similar round or oval wickiups but not as grand as Kennasket's. Adams could not resist examining the scalps he found in several lodges. He was relieved to find that all of the coups counted by Kennasket's flatheaded warriors had been against other redmen. The chief assured him that his tribe did not take white scalps, and never had.

Next, Kennasket showed Adams and his just-waked, bleary-eyed companions over the dancing area which had been prepared by his people for the day's festivities. It was a level, grassy area shaded by large oaks. From the ground, all sticks and stones had been removed and four or five circuslike rings had been staked out for dancing. He also pointed out the fire

rings where meat would be roasted during the celebration.
Adams, following an old—and wise—custom of his when dealing with Indians, admired everything effusively. He almost
broke his rule when he declined Kennasket's invitation to
breakfast, fearing another free-for-all mush dipping. He finally surrendered in fear of alienating the Indian leader's
friendship but was in luck, anyway, since mush held no place
on the menu that morning.

Immediately after breaking their fast, the Indians began
to prepare for the celebration, the men disappearing into
their lodges. Fires were kindled by some of the women who
remained and meat was set out to barbecue. Hardly had the
delightful odor of roasting meat tingled Adams's nostrils when
Kennasket and his men reappeared, handsomely dressed in
furs and skins, and decorated with beadwork, feathers and
painted bark. Tagging in the chief's wake were the villagers
and their guests. Adams estimated that the population of the
rancheria was doubled by the visitors of the day. A number
of the Indians marched into the dance circles and began to
shuffle into a step as others among the red-skinned spectators
began a monotonous but rhythmic chant in lieu of instru-
mental accompaniment.

At midafternoon the dancers took a rest, to eat a dinner
consisting of some 200 game animals, mostly antelope, deer
and bear, and the dreadful mealy stew which Adams had
come to loathe. Kennasket's men had no whiskey, and all
viands had to be washed down with plain water. The Indians, dancers and onlookers alike, fell upon the food as if
they would never see another meal. The squaws were quiet
and unobtrusive but the men showed their enjoyment of the
banquet with whoops of delight as they filled their stomachs
to capacity. Following supper, just as in more civilized climes,
there came after-dinner speeches, starting with an oration by
"Governor" Kennasket himself. He enthralled his audience
with tales of the days and deeds of his warrior youth.

59

Following the banquet was the club dance, a mock battle in which the feather-decked dancers not only brandished war clubs but took vicious swipes at one another's skulls, narrowly—and expertly—missing on each pass. Adams fully expected to see cracked crania as the result of this wild set-to but no blood flowed, for all the participants were chosen for their special skill and dexterity with the dangerous weapon. Toward dusk the dancers ceased and selected archers from among the warriors stepped forward to take their places by showing their skill with the bow and arrow. Most were deadly marksmen and Adams marveled at how easily they split small wood chips at thirty yards and how some of them were able to shoot iron nails from the fingers of their most daring, and trusting, comrades. As the light failed, the bowmen abandoned their competition and the dancers resumed their stomping in the circles. Adams, a few years later, recalled the barbaric scene: "The forms of the plumed and painted Indians, as they passed to and fro in the ruddy glare of the night fires, the dark shadows and the flickering lights on every side, presented a spectacle which will remain indelibly impressed upon my memory."

After a midnight snack, the Indians resumed their dancing. They probably kept at it till dawn but Adams quietly led his companions away in the wee hours of the morning and all fell into their blankets as soon as possible, grateful for the rest of a short night's sleep.

CHAPTER V

COMBINING FORCES

WHEN the hunters finally roused themselves late in the morning, Saxey and Stanislaus felt logy and indisposed from too much celebrating and overeating. So Adams and Tuolumne went off, without them, in search of breakfast. (There was not a scrap of meat in camp.) Dismounting after a short ride, they crept up on four deer but when they were still ninety yards away, one of the wary bucks wrinkled its nostrils, having either seen or sensed the hunters, and the deer prepared to dash with a bracing of muscles. As the watchful buck snorted its alarm, Adams ordered Tuolumne to fire, then followed suit himself. Two of the deer fell and Adams sent Tuolumne ahead to pack them on the mules while he swung around in a beater's semicircle to try to flush more game. He was luckless at this task, however, all the game in the area having been cleared out by the reverberations of the two rifles.

Reaching Tuolumne empty-handed, he found the Indian sitting on a shady slope, fast asleep. Adams hoped to have some fun with the boy. He therefore tried to sneak the mules' reins from Tuolumne's hands but the Digger had wound them tightly around one forearm and all of Adams's tugging only served to awaken him. When Tuolumne saw who it was, he flashed his white teeth in a broad grin and lied that he had learned the Yankee hunter's trick of sleeping with one eye open.

As they were arriving at camp, Saxey made the mistake of asking Adams if he was not quitting just at the time of day when hunting was getting good. The cantankerous Yankee was a little short with him, snapping, "Yes, this *is* the best time of the day to hunt, but you are not the only man whose flesh and blood tire and sleep!"

After a night's rest, Adams's good spirits returned and he spent a lazy day training his pets. He worked particularly with his favorite, Lady Washington, who was now so tame that she followed at his heels like a puppy. Adams decided that he would try to teach her to carry a pack. He filled an old flour sack with sand and lashed it to the back of the shaggy animal. But the Lady made it unmistakably clear that she did not want to become a beast of burden. She snarled, twisted her head about and with her teeth tore a gaping hole in the bag, from which the sand cascaded. Her teacher talked to her firmly, not sparing the rod either, but it did no good. Her Ladyship only grew more furious and even Adams, as short-tempered and stubborn as any grizzly that ever walked like a man, was forced to call off his tutoring for the day. He spent the remainder of the daylight hours training Jackson, the fast-improving black bears, and the wolves.

In a few days, Lady Washington forgot her difference with her master and loped along behind him and the others when they went on a long hike to a spot where Adams planned to build a box trap. She stayed at his side for the whole rugged four miles and shared his lunch with him at noon. En route back to camp, Grizzly sent Saxey, Tuloumne and Stanislaus in a roundabout sweep through the woods to drive before them any game lurking there. In the meantime, he proceeded in a beeline for camp with the tiring and footsore bear. As luck would have it, Adams, not his departed friends, fell in with game. And he had loaned his rifle to Stanislaus! He stumbled on a small group of grazing deer. Normally the hunter would not have tried to bring them down with only a pistol but he felt ambitious that evening and so he crept up on them through thick brush, while Lady Washington lumbered along astern of him. Suddenly, some sixth sense told Adams to stop and retreat. Some corner of his brain flashed an insistent warning that there were more grizzlies in the neighborhood than his companion, although the deer continued to browse placidly, without showing any alarm. Awkwardly, Adams began to crawl backward on hands and knees. His slow retrograde progress was shortly and abruptly halted by a loud snort from Lady Washington, followed by her clicking her teeth in a strange warning.

The hunter, drawing his pistol, turned to find her gazing at the huge, upright form of an old and savage-looking grizzly. Adams hardly knew what to do, but he unwound the chain he had wrapped around Lady Washington's neck and slowly, ever so slowly, began to lead her toward a nearby tree. The monster dropped to all fours and closed with them. Now, Adams did not dare even to move a muscle. He stood stock-still, his pistol at the ready, and tried to stare down the grizzly. But the beast stared back. Adams decided on a desperate gamble, for he could not stay, petrified, in that spot all night. All at once, he rattled the chain sharply, shouted himself hoarse and fired his pistol in the animal's face. It worked! The astounded grizzly turned tail and fled crashing through the brush like a runaway Conestoga. Adams followed up his advantage by pursuing the beast, whooping and hollering and clanking his chain while Lady Washington joined in with her own growls. When the enemy was gone, Adams patted his pet's flank in gratitude. It was the first time that one of his animals had stood by him in the face of danger and he was grateful. On the remainder of the way home, Adams was doubly watchful but nothing untoward happened.

Upon nearing the fire which marked the campground,

Adams fired another chamber of his revolver to alert his comrades of his approach. Saxey and the boys laughed at him, at first, as he strode into the firelight. They accused the old mountain man of having become lost. But he soon set them straight with the tale of his encounter. However, they had an even more interesting story to tell him. When they had reached the camp from the trap, it was to find a fire blazing briskly—and not of their kindling. They gave it little thought until they set to feeding the animals and found that the two black bear cubs were missing. Making a search, they discovered that salt, pepper, jerked meat and powder and ball had also been taken. Adams silently damned himself for taking all of his hands with him to the new trap, leaving his camp entirely unguarded. He hoped that it was just a case of some hunters borrowing stores they needed, but the lack of any note of explanation worried him. And just why had they helped themselves to his two cubs? He could not fathom who his visitors might have been or what their intentions were.

But, at least, Adams could promise himself that he would not be caught napping again. He warned his companions that the stealthy strangers might be hostiles. He ordered them to move their bedrolls back from the light of the campfire so that they would not be sitting ducks for a night ambush. But not even the threat of a war party's arrows or musket balls could impress his men that night, they were so tired from the day's march. Adams had to postpone setting a watch and, instead, decided to depend on the sleepy-looking but wakeful guard at his side, Lady Washington.

Dawn came after a night's rest which was unbroken by any alarm. Adams returned to the trap with Saxey and Tuolumne, leaving Stanislaus in command of the camp. On the way home that night, he and his friends waylaid a herd of thirty to forty antelope and killed three, which they hurriedly packed on one of the mules, for night was falling blackly on he wilderness. Saxey led the loaded mule while riding the other, as Tuolumne and Adams broke trail ahead of him. The Texan, in a short time, became uneasy when a pack of wolves picked up their trail and began to follow them at no great distance. He asked Adams to let him go in front with the mules, since the *lobos* were after the meat he was packing. This was satisfactory with the Yankee hunter, although he assured the half-breed that all the wolves in Washington Territory, together, would not make a formidable force. He and Tuolumne let Saxey pass them and they continued in this order until heavy brush blocked their path. Here, even Adams had to admit that he did not want wolves on his heels in such close quarters, however cowardly they might be. He called a halt and sat down, rifle ready, to discourage the yowling pursuers. But the wolves stopped short and would not come closer than fifty yards. Since they would not approach within accurate rifleshot, Adams ordered his men to fire at their eyes as they flashed in the wan starlight. This barrage frightened the predators away but, before they reached camp that night, there was one more scare in store for Saxey. A mountain lion picked up the trail the wolves had abandoned. It dove at the mules and spooked them but, missing its footing, it dashed away with no more harm done than a claw scratch or two on the pack mule's flank—and considerable fraying of Saxey's already ragged nerves.

The shouts of Indian visitors awakened the hunters next morning and Adams welcomed them to a fire. They turned out to be messengers from Kennasket who brought word of the chief's decision to agree to Adams's offer to swap his two wolf whelps for two horses. After telling them he would visit their chief on the following day, the hunter gave them breakfast. As they chatted, Adams learned from them that another party of white hunters was camped not far away and that they had two black bear cubs with them, "exactly like

Adams's." The Old Yankee thought aloud, "If they are exactly like mine, they must be mine."

Before paying a call on these mysterious visitors, Adams decided to clear his traps. It was a disappointing chore. He found only two coyotes in them. He dispatched the wild dogs of the prairies with his pistol and then made a wide sweep across the plain in hopes of finding some game. To his surprise, he ran into a small herd of buffalo.* And surprised he was, noting, "It is not usual to find buffaloes west of the Rocky Mountains and especially so far west as we now were; but they sometimes stray from their general haunts.... For myself, I knew little of the sport as it is carried on upon the slopes of the Platte and the Upper Missouri, nor was I prepared for such game. But, having a good rifle and considerable experience in the general principles of hunting, I laid my plans according to my circumstances."

Adams sent his friends into an ambuscade while he climbed the hill in a path as straight as a transit line toward the gang of animals. Long before he neared them, they rolled up their tufted tails and turned their rumps to him in an inelegant gesture of *adiós* and thundered off. However, they headed right for the hidden hunters, who fired on them at close range and broke the leg of a cow. "Bravely done!" shouted the New Englander and they joyfully responded with shouts of their own before running to dispatch the beast. But she easily outdistanced the dismounted hunters, even with her gimpy leg. Adams climbed aboard his mule to join the chase. After a mile of hard riding across plain, ravine, knoll and valley at a breakneck gallop, which he encouraged

---

*Adams was so careless with fact that one cannot be sure that he found buffalo at this time—or at all. Perhaps he inserted a buffalo hunt simply to liven his story for his readers. Most historians doubt that he found bison in the area in which he said he found himself, the Palouse. According to his recollections, he did not get to the edge of the real buffalo country until the following summer when he marched from the Sierra Nevada to Bear River, the Rockies, and, finally, the Platte.

by drubbing his mule with a club, he overtook his comrades and stopped them. Shortly, just as Adams had told them would happen, the buffalo cow sagged to the grass, weak from running and loss of blood.

Once she was down, Adams turned his reins over to Tuolumne and tied wreaths of grass around his and Saxey's heads. Then he and the Texan wormed their way forward, hugging the ground. After belly-crawling for a full sixty yards, they were close enough to shoot but could not get a bead on the wounded animal from a prone position. So Adams popped to his feet, swung his rifle butt to his shoulder and gave a shrill whistle. Just as he expected, the buffalo heaved herself to her feet, as if on cue, and stared at him as if trying to decide whether to charge or to run for it. Just as she lowered her massive, curly head to rush him like a Miura bull, Adams broke her train of thought with a well-placed rifle ball. The lead slug flattened against the beast's forehead but only staggered her onrush. Saxey then fired in hopes of stopping her and his ball took her right behind the shoulder, dropping her in the bunch grass. Adams ran forward and slit the animal's throat with his skinning knife.

While dressing out their game, Adams examined the bulletproof skull. For once, Saxey was in the highest of spirits. He celebrated his triumph by claiming all the credit for killing the party's first buffalo. And, for once, the grumpy Adams was not inclined to argue with him. He was content to let his companion have any and all honors. ("His shot was really excellent in itself, and excellently well timed.") After a hurried nine-mile march to camp, all enjoyed succulent buffalo steaks for the first time. They ignored all game, even antelope, on their return, so eager were they to try the choice cuts of bison. While they ate, Stanislaus told Grizzly Adams that a white hunter, a Texan like Saxey, had visited the camp and had expressed the desire to see Adams. The Indian boy could not remember the visitor's name but he did say that the stranger had remarked that he had come overland to California with Adams. The latter tried to recall to mind all of his companions of the Gila Trail but could not guess just which one it might be.

Before turning in for the night, Adams pickled his buffalo robe with saltpeter, alum and a dash of arsenic, which he pulverized and rubbed together over the flesh side of the hide. This treatment arrested putrefaction and kept the skin sweet, soft and pliable. After a couple of days, Adams would unroll the skin, scrape off the greasy part, rub a paste of soaproot on the skin, and let it lie for two days. He would have a handsome buffalo robe as a result of all this tedious work plus a final rubbing with a stone and a smoking of the pelt to prevent insect damage.

Next morning, Adams took Tuolumne with him as he set out for the Indian village with a muleload of buffalo meat and the two whelps, to trade for the horses. Kennasket was delighted with the wolf cubs and willingly gave Adams two fine horses for them—once he had haggled Adams into throwing in, for good measure, a black bear and two sacks of dried venison. Then Kennasket's squaws served dinner to the bargainers. The repast was composed of buffalo meat and bread made of tule root. He found that the women used this reed, so common in California, not only for food but for making woven mats and baskets and also dried it for fuel. He observed their technique in breadmaking. The squaws collected the roots from marshy areas, cut away the rinds and sliced the remainder into chestnut-sized particles which they then sun-dried and ground with *mano* and *metate*. This flour they mixed with a meal made of grass or wild dock seeds. He noted that the recipe always ran about two-thirds tule to one-third grass or burdock meal. This blending gave the little loaves of bread both a good flavor and a firm consistency, neither too crumbly nor too pasty. When baked in the ashes of a campfire, the tiny loaves tasted delectable to Adams.

From the Indian village, Adams and Tuolumne rode to the camp of the mysterious white hunters. They proved to be three Texans, William Frost, a man named Partridge, and a man whom Adams instantly recognized as Kimball, an old forty-niner friend. While Adams asked, rhetorically, just what brought him to those parts, Kimball laughed and said, "Well, to tell the truth, Mr. Adams, I never would have got this far, had it not been for the canteen of water which you gave me on the Colorado Desert." He was referring to the time Adams had shared his canteen with him and a third man as they crossed the most dangerous leg of the Gila Trail to California, the 90 Mile Desert. The third man had died but Kimball always swore that Adams's canteen had saved his life.

Kimball freely admitted helping himself to the black bears, saying that he had figured this would be the surest way of guaranteeing that Adams would look him up. While the Yankee failed to see the humor of this theft, he said nothing and readily accepted Kimball's explanation as well as his invitation to eat and stay the night. The two spent hours beside the fire, talking over their mutual adventures long after their companions had fallen asleep.

The delivery of the bears was made next morning but the chief could not pick one of the cubs over the other so he offered Adams a third horse if he could have both bears. "Agreed!" boomed the hunter. At first, Adams was delighted with his little remuda but soon began to worry over having such valuable property on his hands again after so many months. He began to feel that he ought to post a guard over the animals at night to prevent their being rustled. He had not bothered with the mules because they were hardly worth stealing. But horseflesh was another matter. It was always a temptation to lawless whites or redmen. (He remembered how his French Camp horse herd had been stolen.) Reluctantly, he ordered a constant guard to be kept at night.

The summer season was dying fast so Adams and his partners began to dry a stock of meat for the return trip to California. At this time he determined to find Elk Lake, of which the Indians had spoken. They located it about twenty-five miles from their village and reported great herds of wapiti banding together there. Again taking Tuolumne, who was replacing Saxey, more and more, as his hunting companion, Adams rode out in the early morning light. They reached the lower shore of the lake, where it was edged with a swampy jungle of rushes and tules. In this growth, he found a number of elk and crept up on them through the screening reeds. At his first fire, a big buck dropped to the ground, to be followed by another as Tuolumne's rifle barked. Surprisingly, the other animals—probably because they had never been hunted by riflemen—did not bolt but simply milled in bewildered circles. Adams fired again, breaking the neck of another animal, but the Indian's second shot missed. The survivors finally fled. In the tules lay three elk, more meat than the horses could possibly carry, and Adams cursed his stupidity in not bringing a mule along for packing. He made do by loading three-fourths of an elk on each horse and hiding the remainder under tules. Over the cache he erected a piece of cloth as a flag, both to mark the spot and, like a scarecrow, to frighten away scavenging animals.

A combination of circumstances made their trip back to camp a harrowing one. Saxey and Stanislaus neglected to keep the fire blazing brightly and, with no beacon to guide him, Adams lost his way in the pitch-dark. He and his companion strayed for hours, completely lost, blundering in and out of arroyos. Finally, an exasperated Adams fired his gun. The signal was answered from camp and Adams, quickly noting the direction from which the echoes rolled, led his footsore friend to the campfire. There, he excoriated his other men for their carelessness.

Adams would have preferred to rest the day following their nighttime trek but when Stanislaus said that he doubted that he would ever be able to find the cache of meat at Elk Lake, the Old Hunter resignedly took to the trail again. He took the Indians and the two mules and three horses while the Texan watched over the camp. En route to the cache, they encountered a band of elk, one of which, a 600-pound buck, collapsed after Tuolumne snapped off a shot from horseback. Adams twisted around to congratulate the Indian—"A very skillful feat!" he called it.

While he waited for a return visit from Kimball and his fellow hunters, the Californian checked his traps. He let the others take care of jerking the elk meat. To Adams's disgust, he found his traps, once again, occupied only by coyotes. He shot the pair with his pistol and almost immediately regretted it. Close examination showed him that they were of a species strange to him and the area. They had heavy coats of fine hair. That day, Saxon showed him one of the elk hearts. It had an Indian arrow imbedded in it. (Two years later, at Corral Hollow in California, Adams would kill a deer whose heart bore a small bullet imbedded in it.) He marveled at the stamina of the animals.

Kimball and his men rode in and Adams welcomed them with a real treat—freshly baked bread. The men spent the evening in yarning, then voted to join up in an elk hunt at the lake during the following day.

Elk Lake, on Adams's third visit, was more beautiful than ever. For a moment he stood admiring the body of water surrounded by tree-covered hills and grassy, rolling plains, except for the low side where a jungle of tules, half a mile thick, bounded it. Since it was late in the day when they arrived, the Old Hunter led them toward the rushes to which, he knew, the animals tended to drift from the plains as the day wore on. They liked to stamp in mud and water, cooling themselves on warm days and securing relief from the torturing flies. Leaving the horses at a small wooded creek, the seven men spread out as if in a skirmish line and began to beat their way through the dense tules. Soon they heard the whistling of buck elk. When the animals were in sight, Adams had each man select a target and fire together. At the sound of the volley, the animals rushed about in confusion, crashing through the reeds as if they numbered hundreds of animals. Instead of a great slaughter, however, the hunters found only three dead elk. There were not even bloody trails of other wounded animals. Perhaps it was a good thing, for Adams found that the ground was too boggy to bring the pack animals in for loading. He and his companions had to pack out a quarter of an elk, each, to firm ground and the waiting horses.

Back at camp, the men hoisted the meat into the trees for safekeeping except for one choice cut which furnished them all with a fine meal before they lit their pipes and relaxed around the fire. Again, the men trotted out their best tales of adventure, hunting and wandering, to the accompaniment of a symphony of hooting owls and piping frogs. Finally, the fire sank into its ashes and the tired huntsmen rolled themselves in their blankets and slept.

Dawn found the seven up and on the trail of elk again. They found them grazing on the plains and Adams ordered a surround. He sent Tuolumne and one of his guests around in a circle to get behind the game, then had the rest of his men spread out in a general advance. The confused elk, seeing humans on all sides, foolishly held their ground and Adams's men easily could have killed ten or so of the twenty in the circle. But they were hunting for meat, not for amusement, and Adams called a halt after three animals fell. He let the rest escape. More meat would have been impossible to carry, dress and load. When all of the meat from the three elk was stacked against the trunk of a large tree, it was an impressive sight, reminding the Yankee of nothing less than the old Boston Public Market. The wolves and coyotes were impressed by the meat market, too, and so many predators circled the camp, yelping and howling, that Adams had to mount an all-night guard. He paired off with his old *amigo,* Kimball, and as they whiled the hours of guard duty away with conversation he learned from him that a Boston-bound vessel was lying at Portland, Oregon, scheduled to sail in late September.

As he listened, Adams was struck with an idea. Why not take his animals to the Willamette port and ship them from there, rather than a California port as he had originally planned? He proposed to Kimball that he and his friends join him in a stepped-up hunt and help him get the animals, peltries and bear oil to Portland. Kimball gave the idea very little thought; almost immediately he agreed, saying he certainly owed Adams a lot more than a month's work for saving his life on the Colorado Desert. "Nonsense!" snorted the grizzled mountaineer. "You owe me nothing." He told Kimball that he would pay him and his companions a good wage. Shortly, Kimball talked it over with his fellow Texans. They were ready to hunt with the Californian for one month, then to set out with him and his party for Portland.

While the Texans returned to their camp to close it out, Adams secured the meat at Elk Lake, checked his traps and, with Tuolumne, made a cage out of sugar-pine logs for the wildcat he found trapped. The next day, he killed a gray fox sitting a hundred yards from him (bragging, "I made an excellent shot") and Tuolumne shot a bobcat out of a tree. Shortly after they had skinned out the two animals, they encountered a pair of wolves. Both men fired but missed, for the *lobos* were on a dead run.

The Texans rejoined Grizzly at camp that evening, to plan the ensuing joint hunt. They agreed that each party should be responsible for building one more trap. Adams knew that the darkness would bring wolves, so he disposed his men around the fresh meat when their discussion was finished. Just before midnight, a large, howling pack not only pressed up close to the men but burst into camp and attacked some of the meat. Adams was dumfounded; he had never seen wolves so ravenous that they would dare to invade a camp. He had three of his men fire into the small army of raiders, scattering them. But only one carcass lay stretched out on the ground when the gunsmoke cleared.

Next day, the men separated into their regular parties in order to hunt in different directions. In two more days, Adams's men had finished their trap and the Texans were well along with theirs. During this period, on a deer-hunting excursion, Adams decided to imitate his Digger companions who often fired on game from horseback. When he came upon a deer, Grizzly brought his rifle up and fired without dismounting. The flash and blast of his gun terrified his mount. Somehow, the horse just disappeared from under Adams and the Californian found himself sprawled flat on the ground, unhurt but his hair, beard, eyes and temper full of dust. Gamely, cursing, Grizzly remounted, determined to teach his horse to accept rifle fire from the saddle. He fired again after a short interval and this time brought down an antelope *and* held his seat by digging in his heels and attending carefully to his center of gravity. He brought the antelope meat to camp to bait the new traps.

As they were baiting both traps—the Texans had just put the finishing touches on theirs—the horses pricked up their ears and Grizzly heard the snort of a nearby bear. The Old Hunter waved his friends to a silent stop and scanned the brush in every direction. At last he saw the beast, some 200 yards off. Although it was becoming dark, Adams ordered his men to fire and he, Kimball and Tuolumne blazed away but the grunting beast escaped. The Texans were all for pursuing it through the bushes. "No, it's too dark," said Grizzly, "and there's too much brush in that direction." They protested that they were dying to get a bear but Adams answered, "You just wait a few days and I'll take you to a part of the country where you can have your fill of bear killing."

On the way to camp, Tuolumne wanted to frighten Stanislaus by pretending that he and Grizzly were hostiles. Adams vetoed the idea, although he had been guilty of similar practical jokes. Finally, he saw that this kind of trick was not good for what he tried to explain to the Digger was "that feeling of confidence which ought to exist between hunters." Tuolumne did not get all the reasoning but he got the gist of Adams's speech and knew enough not to cross the cantankerous Californian. Stanislaus had done a fine day's work as camp guard. All the meat was hung up to dry and the already jerked meat was packed in sacks which the Digger had made by sewing antelope skins together with thongs.

That night, around the campfire, the men made further plans for the hunt and march to Portland. Adams reminded the men that everyone would have to work hard, now, to collect as much oil and as many live animals and skins as possible in the single month remaining to them. The hunters replied that they were ready and willing but that Adams would have to be the boss, not only finding the hunting grounds but also organizing and directing the work. Grizzly was nothing loath to accept this position of leadership. ("As it naturally belonged to me," he modestly grunted later, "I willingly accepted.) Knowing how eager were the Texans to hunt something other than deer, antelope and elk, he immediately gave the order for a great buffalo hunt in a valley forty miles to the east. This was a very popular command with everyone and it was greeted by cries of delight by the men squatting around the glowing embers.

CHAPTER VI

BUFFALO DAYS

THE buffalo hunt which Grizzly Adams proposed was not solely for sport; he knew that his men—and the animals—would need plenty of dried meat on the long march west to the Willamette. Buffalo beef would be a pleasant addition to his store of elk, antelope and deer jerky. He took only Kimball, Foster and Tuolumne with him on the hunt itself, so that he would have animals free to pack plenty of meat back to camp. The men took all six horses and both mules. A hard day's ride brought them, at sundown, to the border of the valley which the Indians had told Adams was a buffalo range. It was a beautiful vale and the Old Hunter's sleep that night was brightened by dreams of a rosy future for it. His subconscious mind saw it as a pastoral and agricultural landscape, blocked out with farms and villages and with the floor of the valley dotted with thousands of head of livestock.

Up before the sun, Grizzly soon spied the first gang of buffalo, a group of some eight or ten bison. He ordered his men into the saddle and they tried to surround the small band. Adams fired and brought one animal to its knees with a ball in its shoulder. Another dropped as one of his comrades fired. But the surround was not drawn tightly enough and the rest escaped. However, the two downed animals supplied enough meat to keep the men busy all day. After carrying it

76

to their camp, they had to cut it into strips and hang it on the drying poles, then spread, scrape and treat the hides with saltpeter. Toward evening, Adams suggested another hunt. Everyone, heartily bored with camp chores, agreed. Six or eight miles out they came to a timbered creek with an almost dry channel. Tying their horses in the cover of the timber on the near side, the men crossed the stream bed and, without the slightest difficulty, stalked and killed three huge bulls with just three shots.

Again, so much fresh meat lying about attracted half the lupine population of the area and Adams had to post a sentinel to keep the wolves at bay. Moreover, the men worked through the night in their ravine camp, butchering the bison beef. Their close watch kept losses to zero though a daring coyote sneaked through the shadows to seize a quarter. Before it could drag the meat off, however, Adams gave the thief a blow with a club which broke its back.

The following day, Grizzly repeated his technique of a morning and evening hunt, with butchering chores occupying the middle of the day. This time, the foursome bagged five deer and four foxes in addition to three buffalo. Adams preserved the skins of all the animals and the meat of all except the foxes. Next day, they took three more buffalo in a timbered marsh. This task turned out to be child's play, for the animals mired themselves in the muck and were as easy prey as the animals which the Blackfeet sometimes found similarly immobilized in deep snowdrifts.

On the third day of hunting, the Californian tried to drive a band into the marsh but, perhaps sensing their danger, the shaggy beasts stampeded off to one side, right at the sector guarded by Kimball's friend, William Foster. Foster had longed for a chance to distinguish himself as a hunter so he rashly—foolishly—held his ground, instead of flanking the buffalo. Adams had seen buffalo collide with trees in their stubborn refusal to be thrown off course in a stampede and

77

his heart sank as he saw Foster try to stem their rush. Suddenly, man and horse were down, in a cloud of dust. Adams and the others ran to the man's aid. They found Foster alive and, miraculously, not even seriously hurt, although painfully battered by hooves. Grizzly treated him with what he called his water cure—tearing a blanket into strips with which, soaked in cold water, he bound up the victim of the mishap like a mummy.

Leaving Foster at their ravine rendezvous, Adams, Tuolumne and Kimball continued the hunt and though Adams's rifle ball glanced off one beast's thick forehead, his comrades wounded two others which they quickly finished off. On the fifth day of the hunt, it was Adams's turn to follow Foster into trouble—and the Old Hunter had to admit that it was his own fault. He afterwards blamed his misfortune on overconfidence in his hunting skill. Adams and his three companions (Foster had rejoined them already) pursued a large band of buffalo into the natural trap of the swampy area. The soft going made mounted pursuit impossible, of course, so all four men leaped to the ground and plunged deeper into the marsh. Before long, the heavy beasts which they were pursuing were mired like logs in the mud and it was no chore for the hunters to slaughter four of them. The last bull lay a little beyond the others so Adams, putting aside his empty rifle, set out to kill it with his bowie knife. (Later, he candidly admitted, "I was actuated in this by a foolish desire of exhibiting my bravery.") The beast quickly made a fool of the Old Hunter. As Adams came up to the animal, knife drawn for the fatal thrust into its throat, the angry-eyed buffalo heaved itself partially out of its mucky bed. The beast's lunge knocked Adams off his feet and although he held on to his knife he was not able to ply it. The curved horns and massive, curly head of the animal were soon pressing him inexorably into the soft mud. This was no laughing matter—Adams found himself in great danger of being suffo-

78

cated in the filthy mire. The ooze was so soft that the butting of the beast did not break any bones but deeper and deeper he sank. He was just about convinced that he had not only found his grave but his gravedigger, to boot, when Kimball ran up, brought the muzzle of his gun within inches of the animal's body, and fired. The impact and shock of the rifle ball caused the buffalo to jerk its head up. Quickly, Adams scrambled to his feet.

The men spent two days drying meat and curing hides, for Foster and Tuolumne had killed two buffalo about the time Adams was being pummeled into the mud by Number Four. They made only one more hunt and kept only the skins of the three animals they killed. On the eighth day, they packed for their return to the main camp. The hunters had to leave a good deal of meat behind but they still loaded sixteen sacks with jerky and carried off, also, twenty buffalo robes, six or eight deerskins and ten antelope skins, plus sixteen valuable fox pelts.

When Adams's hunters rendezvoused with the other men they found that the latter had done quite well, too, killing a grizzly and taking alive two black bear cubs and three wolves. They had also killed eighteen deer, six antelope, four gray foxes and three raccoons, so there was no shortage of either meat or pelts in camp. That night, by the fire, the men swapped stories of their adventures. Adams's muddy close shave won all prizes for general interest.

The next three days were very successful ones for the huntsmen, who killed antelope, foxes, elk and a grizzly. Another grizzly bear awakened them in camp one night and Adams had to stop the impulsive Foster from chasing off into the night after the departed visitor. Next morning, Foster would have his chance.

The men were out hunting when they came upon a large female grizzly with two cubs. Foster was beside himself for a shot and although Adams warned him to stay with the others until they could reach a wooded knoll beyond the bear, Foster advanced directly at the she-bear, saying he could kill a bear as easily as a buck deer. Adams could do nothing with him except to pry a promise out of him that he would not fire until the others had reached the cover of the knoll. But before they reached the hillock they heard the report of a rifle and the terrifying roar which Adams knew so well as the warning grizzlies gave as they charged at men.

Adams hurried to help Foster. He was just in time to see his companion being dragged out of a tree by one foot, clamped in the maw of the wounded brute. Many times he had lectured his hunting companions to lie deathly still if ever they fell into the power of a grizzly, however badly they might be mauled. But poor Foster forgot to play possum and shrieked for help and tried to struggle away. Adams rushed at the bear with his knife poised, mainly to attract the beast's attention from the fallen hunter, but the monster ignored him and tore at Foster's body, killing him instantly. Mother bear and cubs then became frantic with fury and bloodlust and although Adams carefully placed a ball behind the beast's shoulder, she only fell momentarily. As she clambered to her feet to charge him, Adams reloaded and sent a second ball to the base of her ear, which put an end to her. Now the good-sized cubs took up the fight. Kimball, Partridge, Saxon and Tuolumne all fired but only one of the bears dropped. The other, wounded, still showed fight—plenty of it—and since all the rifles were empty the hunters braced themselves, knives in hand, for its attack. The large cub charged Tuolumne and knocked him sprawling before he could make a stroke with his skinning knife. But Kimball and Adams leaped on the animal and dug their knives into its heaving sides to dispatch it. Tuolumne, aside from bites and scratches, was unhurt.

Grizzly sent Partridge and Saxey to the headquarters camp for a pickax and shovel and when they returned the men dug a grave for Foster under an oak tree near Elk Lake. Adams

asked Kimball to say a prayer, which he did. After a heart-
felt "Amen!" by Adams, the hunters lowered the body of
their comrade, wrapped in his blanket, into the five-foot-
deep grave. They placed sticks atop the corpse, threw in a
layer of leaves, then filled the grave with earth and heaped
up a small mound on top of it. At the head and foot of the
grave they placed a smoothed slab and carved a headstone on
the tree above Foster's last resting place, giving his name,
the date, and an account of the sad manner of his passing.
As they gathered up their tools and jackets to head back to
camp, Adams mused, "Poor Foster! He was an unfortunate
but bravehearted and willing-handed man, and we had all
begun to love him. May he rest peacefully in the lonely grave
to which our rough but friendly hands consigned him."

Much saddened by Foster's death, the hunters nevertheless
kept to their schedule of hunting and trapping although they
had little heart for it. Besides killing many deer, antelope
and foxes, they caught several fawns, four fishers, two panthers, a brown bear and cub, two black wolves, four black
foxes, two black bear cubs, and two white wolves—the first
of the kind that any of them had ever caught. They caught
a grizzly, too, but killed it in the trap. The larger animals
they dragged to camp with lassos; the smaller beasts, including the mountain lions, they caged and packed to camp by
muleback. Adams and Kimball experimented with armor in
handling the bear cubs. The two men wrapped their lower
arms in elm bark and while their friends hoisted the trapdoor, they entered, seized and bound the cubs, with hardly
a scratch.

Because Adams was a unique kind of hunter, seeking all
manner of animals instead of just hunting those with edible
flesh or marketable pelts, he had to make his camp a center
for a series of traplines and hunts radiating out in all directions and into all kinds of different country. He had learned
that buffalo liked grassy prairies, antelope the higher, drier

plains, and elk the moister, lower ground. Cougars preferred heavy timber but foxes chose rugged brush country. Adams's "bear grounds" were in a hilly area which was only thinly timbered but which was densely covered with brush, much like the chaparral of California's Sierra foothills and Coast Range.

Five days after Foster's burial, Grizzly led his men to the bear range. They came upon two old animals and two nearly full-grown youngsters industriously digging up a hillside. Not wanting a repetition of the Foster incident, Adams turned to his comrades to sharply demand a promise that Kimball and Partridge would follow his orders *exactly*. Receiving their promises, he directed them to climb the hill above the bears and to fire on them. Carefully, he spelled out the next step. Should they be attacked, they were to circle around the hill, obliquely, and reascend the hill toward the top. (Adams knew that bears found it difficult to follow a hunter in an angling, uphill course.) If they had to, the men were to climb the trees on the summit.

Everything seemed to go well at first. Both of the young bears were wounded at the first fire. The older animals rushed the hunters. Adams ordered everyone into the trees, knowing that full-grown grizzlies rarely climbed after men perched in the boughs over their heads.

The two grizzlies ran back and forth from tree to tree, giving the men plenty of time to reload while aloft. Adams fired at the female under his perch, while Kimball took the male which prowled and snarled under his tree. Both beasts, badly wounded, lumbered off toward one of the cubs, now lying dead. (The other had disappeared.) Reloading again, the men dropped to the ground and fired another volley in the growing darkness. The shots had no effect and the old bears escaped while Adams organized a rude camp for the night in the dense chaparral in order that they might make a dawn start on the bloody trail of the wounded animals. He set a watch that night, in case one of the bruins should return for revenge.

Grizzly became impatient when nothing occurred and a moon showered cold light on the landscape. He busied himself examining the animals' trail. It was so bloody that Adams convinced himself that the badly wounded grizzlies could not have gone far. So he loudly announced that he was going into the thicket after them. His comrades declined to accompany him, pointedly reminding him of his words of caution in regard to grizzlies. In fact, they said he was quite mad to even think of crawling through the underbrush in the middle of the night on the trail of a painfully wounded pair of grizzly bears.

Adams struck a pose, carefully placing the butt of his hunting rifle on the ground and asking, quietly but theatrically, "Gentlemen, was it bears you came to hunt?" It was not a rhetorical question; he waited for an answer. They admitted that it was, indeed, bears. "Well, then," continued the Old Hunter, "I am astonished to see you falter. We have lost a companion, it is true; but that is no reason why bears cannot be hunted with safety. Here we have several fine ones wounded and, without a doubt, disabled. We can find them without much search. It is safer and easier to follow these than to hunt up others; and, besides, it is cowardly to falter at this stage of the business."

Finally, his head-shaking comrades said that they were ready to follow him. Dropping to his hands and knees, Adams led them on to the tunnel-like, bloody trail of the bears in the thicket. Four hundred yards of stooping or crawling brought them to the bank of a dry creek, overgrown with chaparral. They halted, talked over their next move, then followed the creek bed downstream. Only a hundred yards down, Adams, ahead, spied the old she-bear lying on her side. From her position he felt sure that life had flickered out of her body so he playfully hopped on top of the carcass to

83

throw a little scare into his comrades. He posed himself there as if he were holding the beast down with main strength. As his friends turned a curve in the creek and came into sight, Adams shouted to them for help. He soon enlightened his startled companions as he laughed loudly and jumped down to examine the carcass. He found that the bear was shot through the heart, bowels and head but that several rifle balls had failed to penetrate the layer of fat which underlay her tough, matted, hide.

Down the creek went the hunters, still directed by the red stains of blood on the sandy bed. It was a good mile before they discovered the two remaining bears. Both were in their den and alive. Adams told his men to fire without losing a moment if he needed help, then crept to a nearby bush, took off his fur cap and drew deliberate aim on the big male. The rifle sent a ball straight to the animal's heart. The grizzly just rolled over, growled, and died. The cub started to rise but was cut down by Adams's companions.

A few days later, the party had an even more exciting time in this bear country. From a tree, Adams scanned the countryside and directed his men like a field commander. He had them take positions to surround a she-grizzly and two cubs. He then descended and took up his place in the advance, crawling through a valley of wild oats. Suddenly, Adams heard a gunshot. He rose to his feet at once and saw the old lady rushing at Saxon, who was trying desperately to reload. Adams shouted to him, "Climb a tree!" As he was doing so, Kimball fired and hit the animal in one buttock, spinning her around. But now she charged him and Kimball, unluckily, was far from any climbable tree. Adams ran to help him but Kimball managed to find and climb an oak so the Old Hunter ducked behind a bush before the bruin saw him.

In his hurry, Kimball had dropped his unloaded rifle and when Adams saw that the grizzly was about to break the standing rule for older bears by climbing the oak, he decided that he had better play his hand in the game. He fired but his shot, though it took her in the neck, only maddened her and she continued her climb as Kimball discharged chamber after chamber of his revolver in her face, without effect. Adams, hurrying his reloading, yelled to Kimball to take courage and to use his knife like a man. His gun reloaded, Adams ran to the very foot of the tree, got directly underneath the belly of the bear and placed a ball just under one foreleg. The grizzly rolled over onto a limb, hung there a moment, then crashed to earth. Adams immediately sprang upon her, plunging his knife repeatedly into her heart.

When he looked up to see Kimball, Adams found that he had climbed to the very top of the tree. As usual, Adams unleashed his temper and bawled him out for not coming down —to help him—instead of heading skyward. Kimball said that he was sorry but that his only thought had been escape from the jaws of the grizzly. While Adams was chastizing Kimball, Saxey came up and Old Grizzly gave him a piece of his mind, too, for having "consulted his own safety more than my danger." By moonlight, the men captured the cubs by building a brush hut over the body of the mother bear. When the cubs entered the rude corral, Adams and his men sprang upon them, wrestling and tying them, not without suffering some bloody scratches.

Some days later, Grizzly Adams rode to the Indian village to engage horses and men to help him move his menagerie to civilization. As he explained his plan to Kennasket, he said that he would strike a great bargain. When he heard the word bargain, the chief smiled significantly and held out one arm, bandaged wrist to elbow. "White man, very good," he said, but added, "But white man's bargains—very bad." Adams learned that one of the black bear cubs had bitten the chief badly. Grizzly answered that if the bears were so bad he was willing to buy them back. However, when Kennasket asked him whether this meant that he would return the horses, the Old Hunter speedily changed the subject. Finally, Adams was able to have thirty horses and six Indians for the 300-mile-long trip to Portland, though Kennasket feared trusting so much of his horseflesh among the white men of the city. Adams agreed to furnish saddles and trappings and to give Kennasket two sacks of dried meat for every horse and six fawns and a young elk for the loan of the braves.

Grizzly led one more buffalo hunt, to secure meat to pay off the chief. He then spent several days making saddles out of boughs fastened with wooden pegs and covered with elkskin. By the time these were completed, the camp looked like an Oriental bazaar or caravansary from the multitude and variety of marked and numbered packs strewn all over the clearing.

Finally, payment was made to Chief Kennasket and, one noon, Adams led a bizarre column of twelve men, thirty-six horses, two mules and a mobile zoological garden of wild animals out of his campsite. The animals which were not amenable to being led or driven were packed in panniers on horses or mules. The first night's camp was at Kennasket's lodge, where Adams bought back, for six packs of dried meat and four wolfskins, the two bears he had sold him earlier. The chief did not forget to ask after the puppy he had given Adams and was gratified when Grizzly showed him that the whelp was in his caravan. During the conversation, Kennasket also asked Adams what he was going to give him as a going-away present and remembrance of the Great White Hunter. Adams apologized that he had only wild beasts but that he would be happy to offer the chief his choice of them. Kennasket chose one of the white wolves.

Next day, Adams reorganized his cavalcade. In the lead he placed five horses packed with thirty-five buffalo robes, then four horses carrying bearskins and several grizzly skulls. Next came two horses with deerskins, two with antelope skins, one with pelts of foxes and of other small animals. Seven were packed with dried meat for the animals, one bore two boxed bear cubs and another bore boxed, untamed wolves. One mule carried baskets holding foxes and fishers; the other was packed with blankets, tools and camp gear. All of the horses, even those the men rode, carried dried meat for the men. In a small, crazy herd driven by his men came six bears, four deer, four wolves, four antelope, two elk and the Indian dog. This ragtag herd resembled shipwrecked survivors of Noah's cargo as they straggled and quarreled their way west.

Two Indians, normally, rode in the van as scouts and guides, followed by the packhorses tended by four Indians. Next came Adams himself. Kimball, Partridge, Saxon, Stanislaus and Tuolumne brought up the rear. Sometimes, however, Kimball abandoned the rear guard and joined Adams in the very point of the column but, since they did not know the trail, they left the choice of route to the Indian guides. The wild animals tired easily on the road and Adams found he usually had to camp by midafternoon. But, when they reached a place called Little Rock, he found that they had made twenty miles that day.

At Little Rock there was a stone ledge from which a spring fed a stream which flowed west. Adams had the animals unloaded there, then arranged the packs into an enclosure and posted a two-man guard with one of the two men, always, a member of his own party. It was not so much that he feared treachery from Kennasket's men but he was not sure how reliable they would be and, in any case, he was going to take no chances with his precious cargo.

On the fourth day out, Adams found the horses' backs were chafed and swollen so he had his party lay by for a few days while the animals' sores were doctored with water and soaproot. He would have liked to stay longer but a shortage of water, combined with his caravan's exposure to night predators, persuaded him to move on five miles to Yellow Rock. There he found good feed, water and hunting in a grassy valley enclosed by high hills covered with oak, pine and cedar. Adams kept his party there three days, resting up alongside the little stream which etched its meandering way through the valley.

The afternoon after leaving the colored rock campsite, Adams averted what would have been, easily, the most historic and colorful stampede in the whole history of the Far West. He diverted a band of fifteen to twenty horses which three Indians were driving too close to his menagerie's line of march for comfort. After turning their horses, he held a powwow with the Indian herders and learned that there was a large *rancheria* about twenty-five miles ahead of him, on a fishing stream. Adams took the trouble to remind his visitors that his party was bound for the white settlements, with an idea to discouraging any ideas they might possibly have of attacking his party. He wanted them to know that Government vengeance would be assured should anything happen to him. He also set a close guard over his camp that night, but nothing occurred to disturb his, or anyone else's, slumber. He deliberately avoided the village so that he would not have to share his meagering rations. After passing through some densely wooded country, he reached the upper valley of the Columbia River and camped on its bank.

Grizzly tried hard to find a ford, swimming his horse across to the far bank and poking with a pole to try to find bottom all the way across. While he sought a crossing, he let his men fish for perch. When he came back to the campfire, where fresh fish were frying on flat stones greased with bear oil, it was to tell his men that fording was impossible and that they would have to build a raft. Working all the following day, they completed the craft, about twenty feet long and ten feet wide. It was made of pine logs floored with planks of split cedar which were secured with wooden pins. He figured that it could carry all the animals and baggage across in just three trips.

That night, seven Indians blundered into camp. Adams hurried his party out again and prepared to cross immediately, fearing that he might wake up next morning to find his party surrounded. He left the lading to his comrades while he tied lariats together and fastened one end to a tree on the bank. Then, mounting his horse, he crossed with the line to the opposite bank and tied it to a tree which he found there.

Adams ordered the men to cast off and, standing in the bow, captain of a vessel for the first time in his life, he directed his eight oarsmen to row like fury. They propelled the clumsy craft with their sweeps along the line of the "cable" and, working hard and well, scarcely speaking a word, brought the raft to a safe landing on the far shore. It took little time to unload and to make another round-trip voyage. The third and last passage was begun at daylight. This time, the wild animals were very restive and Adams had to abandon his bow position as captain and pilot in order to take up a post in the midst of the bears, to quiet them. But the more he tried to soothe the beasts, the worse-behaved were these reluctant sailors. In the middle of a growling, churning, chaos the guide rope broke and the raft began to float free. The current caught at it and soon was sweeping it downstream at a rapid clip. Lady Washington and a black bear jumped overboard but swam after the raft. The men, who labored and swore like Trojans, by dint of great effort were able to bring the raft to the far bank safely and only a quarter of a mile below their actual destination.

It was now quite impossible to ferry the horses over, of course, so Adams jumped back into the river and swam to them. Ordering Tuolumne to take the lead, he mounted up and led the other Indians into the water, driving the herd before them. All but two horses crossed safely. The pair which perished panicked and forgot to keep their noses high. They drowned and their bodies floated down the river. It took a whole day to sort and dry things out before Adams could move on, but he was grateful to fate for letting him off so easily on the dangerous Columbia crossing.

The next obstacle was a waterless stretch of country in which the guides lost their way. So Adams and Kimball had to forge ahead, just as in gold rush days, to try to find either water or the lost trail. Adams had no luck in finding either, but Kimball came upon water, at least, and the column was able to move up to rest and refresh itself. The "road" to Oregon was simply a narrow trail used by Indians going to the Columbia fisheries. Several days were wasted in a vain search for the trail after it was lost by the Indian guides, then Adams directed Kimball to take one of the scouts with him and to return to the river crossing to pick up the route again there. He ordered the Texan to blaze trees along their path. Luckily, the two men found the trail long before they were as far as the river and had only a fifteen-mile hike to camp to make to report their success.

Wilder and wilder grew the rugged country until the caravan had to climb over a mountain which the Indians called the Humpback. It was a difficult ascent but Adams felt rewarded for the effort when he reached the ridge and found a splendid view falling away before his eyes. Looming above the wilderness were the inspiring, beautiful white peaks of Mount Rainier and Mount St. Helens. The men descended the far side of the mountain to a stream where they camped for the night.

Their night's rest was broken by an alarm and the report of a stampede of their remuda, supposedly by rustling Indians. The horses had, indeed, broken away from their pickets but Adams, reconnoitering on the dead run, rifle in hand, decided that they had been spooked by a wild animal, or animals, and not by horse-thieving redskins. His theory was proven next morning when panther tracks and blood spatters were found. Following the catamount's spoor, the men came upon the carcass of one of the horses, its neck much gnawed by the mountain lion. The country was so broken that the horses were not encouraged to flee far and Adams's prediction that they would be found bunched in ravines proved to be a good prophecy. They eventually recovered all but two animals, and encamped at the stream once again.

Two more days of rock and mountainous country brought Adams's company to a beautiful, parklike valley. Another pair of days of travel and they came in sight of the wide lower valley of the Columbia. Adams struck the river near the Cascades, a few miles below the ferry. The grizzly hunter proceeded to the ferry where he had a heated quarrel with its proprietor, a Pennsylvanian named Hall gifted with a noticeable lack of brotherly love. He demanded more than $100 to ferry Adams and his zoo across the river in his boat. Adams offered to pay his toll in meat, pelts or animals, since he had no money. Hall refused. Next, Adams suggested that he take one of the horses in payment. Again the obstinate ferryman demurred. Grizzly was beginning to heat up now, and he told the Pennsylvanian that he was going to cross, like it or not, and that he would use his boat. The volleys of words exchanged on the banks of the Columbia grew angrier and, at last, Hall turned and strode toward his cabin. Adams took this action to mean that the ferryman was going for a weapon. Grizzly brought up his rifle and strongly advised Hall to stop. He did so. After more bickering, the fellow gave in and offered to ferry Adams's party in exchange for the best horse in the train.

Adams seized on this weakening stand of the Pennsylvanian and, pointing, said, "There stands a horse worth $175 in any market. If you would like to take him, good and well. If not, it cannot be helped." The grumbling ferryman replied, "I suppose if I do not take him, I will get nothing." Adams shot back a sharp, corrective, rejoinder, "I *know* that you will get nothing!"

The ill-natured fellow, as cranky as Adams himself, finally

ferried the party over in two divisions and Adams was able to lead his party downriver through well-settled country. Here they were the objects of all eyes. By evening, they were within sight of Portland. Adams halted to set up camp in a grove of trees. Passing a few days in the city, Grizzly was able to arrange for the shipment of his animals, skins, oils and curios on the bark *Mary Ann*, bound for Boston. He hired a man to sail with her, to look after his wild cargo and keep the animals well fed and watered. Besides the meat Adams had provided, the bark bore a cargo of salmon which could be dipped into for feed, so the hunter had no worry about his animals reaching the East safely. At the last moment, Adams decided to keep his favorite, Lady Washington, with him.

Securing an advance upon the credit of his brother, Adams was able to pay off Saxon, Kimball and Partridge. He gave presents to the Indians who had helped him and the party broke up. Kennasket's braves took the horse herd back to the village in eastern Washington Territory. Saxey decided to stick with Kimball and Partridge for a while in Oregon.

So it was that Adams, accompanied only by Stanislaus, Tuolumne and Lady Washington, set out south along the Willamette Trail for California. The trip was uneventful except for the crossing of the snowy Siskiyou Range. But even in the rugged Siskiyous, Adams's Sierra experience had well prepared him for winter weather and he and his little group dropped safely into the Yreka Valley and made their way south, and then east, to Grizzly's permanent "home" on the headwaters of the Tuolumne River.

CHAPTER VII

VALE OF AHWANEE

IT was October 1853 when Adams's party returned to his old Tuolumne River permanent camp, with Lady Washington straggling behind as a reluctant rear guard. To his disgust, Adams found that his old home had been visited by whites and vandalized. The door, over which he had labored so long, was broken off, his clay "plaster" was peeled away from the walls in places, and a number of the poles of the frame were out of joint. And everywhere were the scars of senseless hatchet strokes.

Grizzly wasted a little breath on the white hunters, spewing epithets on them for their wanton destruction. But he quickly cast them from his mind and set about making things aright. Luckily, his tools and all his other property of value, which he had cached in a cave, were untouched. With the help of the two Indian boys, it took him no time at all to fix up a warm and weathertight home and to lay in a store of dried grass for the horses.

Once the camp was refitted, Adams dropped down to William J. Howard's Ranch to pick up his wagon. But he decided to leave it there in Howard's care, along with his mules, till spring. He wanted the animals to fatten up on the good pasturage of the lower-down ranch because he intended to use them to make a visit to the Rocky Mountains during the summer of 1854.

On the way to and from the ranch, Grizzly passed the village to which Tuolumne and Stanislaus belonged. The chief of the tribe asked after the youths so, once he was back in camp, the grizzly hunter fitted the duo out with new buckskins and gave them leave for the winter. He made each of them a present of a horse and bade them good-bye. The young men promised to return before spring should break, ready to accompany Adams to any corner of the globe he might choose.

With only Lady Washington and his pet dog, the hunter wintered snugly in the Sierra. He busied himself repairing his traps, constantly accompanied by the kindly-tempered grizzly in all his tasks and excursions. Hunting one day, at Bell's Meadows some five miles from camp, Adams killed a fat buck and began to pack it out. He found that the carcass was too heavy for him so he decided to see if the Lady, trained to carry small packs in Washington Territory, might be able to tote the buck. He split the deer in half and bound one side on the bear's back while he shouldered the other. He half expected to see her roll over on top of her load, not that such an action would ruin the meat for bait or bear food. However, Lady Washington stood stock-still, then tried to paw off the load. Next, she twisted her head so as to catch part of the pack with her teeth. She was about to tear it to shreds when Adams dissuaded her with a rap or two with a cudgel. Although she growled, she desisted. She followed him for a short distance but then rolled over and over to shake off the annoying burden. When Adams called to her sharply and cuffed her, she clambered to her feet and followed him again. One more time Lady Washington tried to roll her pack off but, at last, gave in to Adams's authority and carried her load to camp. A few days later, when Adams trapped a large grizzly and decided to stand guard on the trap all night to prevent an escape, Lady Washington obligingly carried his blankets. She stayed with him at the trap for several nights until he could transfer his catch to a secure cage. A week or two later he caught a female grizzly and two yearlings. He took the adult bears and the cubs to Sonora, where he got a good price for them and was enabled to stock up with grub for the winter. At this time, Tuolumne and Stanislaus rejoined him,* to keep him and Lady Washington company.

As winter deepened, the snow line descended to lower elevations, game grew scarce, and the traps seldom took any toll. When the crust hardened, Adams was able to travel easily over the snow on snowshoes but had to treat Tuolumne for frostbite after one of his hunting trips. On another hunt, Adams and Stanislaus were caught by a storm and forced to take shelter under a pine. It was so cold that Adams gave shivering Stanislaus his blanket and crawled up against Lady Washington's shaggy side, where he spent a cozy night. He also found that she could be persuaded to haul a sledge; so, to his surprise, grizzly bears were shown capable not only of being beasts of burden but even draft animals.

As the snow line began to reverse itself, retreating up toward the mountain peaks, Grizzly decided that he wanted a look at Yosemite Valley, the fabled vale called Ahwanee by the Indians. According to Adams, he spent many days hunting there with Solon (or was it Saxon?) and Tuolumne, taking two-thirds of their prizes and leaving the rest to his hunting companions. He got a horse, as well as his mules, from Howard and they set off in a southeast course with Lady Washington and a greyhound bitch which he bought at Howard's. Three days of difficult, up-and-down travel brought them to the brink of the valley. Although Adams felt that the grandeur was beyond the power of human de-

---

* According to Adams's 1860 memoir, a man named Solon, from Sonora, joined him at this time also, and was in on the capture of the bear which Adams named Ben Franklin. On the other hand, the version which he prepared for P. T. Barnum gave his companion not as Solon but his old hunting companion, Saxon or Saxey, whom he said he had left in Portland.

scription, he made a game attempt himself, writing his impression for T. H. Hittell:

"The first view of this sublime scenery was so impressive that we were delayed a long time, as if spellbound, looking down from the mountain upon the magnificent landscape far below. It is vain to attempt to convey the effect produced by those giant and picturesque cliffs three thousand feet high, that romantic valley-bottom with its green carpet and silvery stream, and those groves of trees, which are formed and placed as if a skillful artist had disposed them to portray the essence of romance. It is vain to attempt with words alone, to convey the impressions produced upon the mind by such an enchanting sight; magnitude may be imagined, beauty may be conceived, but the breadth and scope of these rocks, the tempered tints of these distances, the influence of these sublime forms inclosing within their compass lawns and groves and grassy banks, presenting at every turn new and unimagined splendors—all these must be seen and felt, to be fully comprehended. . . . Who could ever forget those stupendous cliffs, with their fit associates, the tapering evergreens? Or the greenswards and oak and cottonwood groves of the valley?"

Pitching their camp in the wide, grassy floor of the valley, the men hunted bear and deer, with great success, for several days. In this hunter's Eden, the greyhound presénted Adams with a litter of pups, one of which would grow up to be Rambler, his companion of many hunts and a good friend of the noble grizzly, Ben Franklin.

Grizzly discovered a bear's den on the headwaters of the Merced River. He invited his white companion, whether Solon or Saxon, to join him in killing the adult animal, or animals, in order to capture the cubs which were bound to be hidden inside the cave. His comrade begged off, wanting no part of an attack on grizzlies "in their own castle." This was satisfactory with Adams, in any case, since he still preferred

When artist Charles Nahl sketched a grizzly bear for the California state flag, his model was one of Old Adams's brutes. (The earlier, crude animal of the Bear Flag Republic's banner was called a pig by the Mexican-Californians.)

As stubborn as he was fearless, Adams went right into the lairs of wolves after them. He simply refused to be outwitted by any animal. He described one cave entry in these terms: "The wolf, notwithstanding his cowardly disposition, is an ugly fellow to deal with in close quarters, and many men in this situation would have been very willing to leave him alone; but I determined to give him fight."

Although the Humboldt Mountains of Nevada provided Grizzly Adams with some good hunting, especially of panthers or mountain lions, he never did come upon the fabled "purple panthers" of the desert mountains— nor has anyone else.

Grizzly Adams had little or no trouble with the Indians, although he was often completely at their mercy. His secret was fair dealing and respect. When Chief Kennasket of Washington Territory presented him with a virtually worthless pup, as a present, Adams feigned the greatest of pleasure in order not to offend the Chief.

Before Old Adams tried traps on grizzlies, he used a less effective technique of shooting the adult animals of a bear family, and then lassoing the cubs, which were always reluctant to leave their parents, dead or alive.

Grizzly Adams's one weakness was carelessness. So skillful did he become as a hunter that he sometimes underestimated his animal adversaries. Such was the case when he tried to dispatch a bull buffalo, mired in a swamp, with only a knife. The bison nearly drowned him in the muck before a hunting companion saved his life.

In one tight spot, Adams was able to chase off a grizzly by shouting at the top of his lungs, waving his hat and rattling his pet bear's chain. What he never forgot about the incident, however, was the fact that his bear, Lady Washington, stood by him ready to fight off the wild intruder of her own species.

One of Adams's close escapes came in combat with a bull elk, an animal not normally considered dangerous at all. But the wounded buck took him by surprise, striking him with both front hooves and knocking his knife to the ground. Luckily, a cut and bruised Adams was able to draw his pistol and finish off the maddened animal.

Of all the many animals which he encountered in his wanderings, Adams thought the feral cattle of the California Coast Range to be the most terrifying in appearance, even worse than grizzlies. However, the wild longhorns were far more likely to flee him than was *Ursus horribilis.*

Grizzly Adams and his best friend, Ben Franklin, taking a *paseo* in the Sierra Nevada of California in the 1850's.

to hunt alone. He collected together three or four days' provisions, cleaned his pistol and rifle, sharpened his knives and, packing his blankets and food on a mule, headed for the cavern.

The hunter found the bear's lair in a narrow ravine between two hills covered with thickets of thorny chaparral and occasional junipers and scrub pine or cedar. He had no trouble finding the den about fifty feet above the stream bed. The pile of fresh dirt at its mouth was as big as a fair-sized glory hole's dump. Climbing a nearby tree, he spied out the area and found a good hiding place in a clump of junipers about one hundred yards from the cave. Adams built a fire where he had left his mule, then returned to his blind in the junipers and began a patient watch which lasted all night, despite the cold. He heard the barking of cubs during the night but otherwise the arroyo was a dreary and silent place.

When the sun rose, a cramped, stiff and cold Adams decided to fire off his rifle, to see if it might flush the bear and also to replace the damp charge with a fresh load. He was prudent enough to climb a tree as soon as he heard growling but soon it was quiet as a tomb. After a while, Adams dropped down to the ground again. The little cañon remained still till noon.

Lunching back where he had left his mule, he refreshed himself at a spring, then resumed his watch. The afternoon passed dully and he stole a little nap, for only a few chirping birds and soaring buzzards, high above, seemed to be stirring. Adams built another fire for his mule that evening and settled down at his post for a second shivering night. It was *very* unlikely that a grizzly parent would hole up for two nights in a row without going out to prowl about for food. Sure enough, during the night an adult female grizzly appeared. He fired his rifle and was rewarded with, at least, a glimpse of the bear's head and forepaws at the mouth of the stronghold. He also heard plainly the yelping of her cubs. But apparently the dam's keen nose picked up his scent and although she did not see him, she refused to come any farther but, instead, retreated into the bowels of the cave.

For a third night, Adams prepared for a vigil. He chose a new blind some forty yards across the ravine from the den after feeding his mule and eating a lonely dinner himself. Excitement had kept him awake two days and nights, but now his body cried for sleep and although he fought it, sleep overtook him and held him for hours. In fact, it was nearly morning when the screech of a panther on the hill startled him awake. For a moment, he was rattled and terror-stricken as his mind clawed its way out of deep sleep. Then he realized that it was only a puma. "What a fool am I," thought Adams to himself, "to be startled by the cry of a panther, a cowardly brute which would dare not stand face to face and fight with a man, while here I am, inviting a combat with a grizzly bear, the savagest beast that ranges the forest!"

Working up his courage again, Adams decided to rouse the grizzly. He could not keep watch for a fourth night. After stuffing his cap full of green twigs as camouflage, he uttered a terrific shout. (He had often "yelled" grizzlies to their feet; perhaps he could roar one out of its den.) There was a booming in the side of the hill like a hidden locomotive making steam and the furious grizzly burst out of the cave and reared up on her hind legs to peer angrily about in every direction. Adams stood as still and silent as a fence post in his hiding place and, shortly, the bear dropped to her haunches again. As she turned, perhaps to re-enter the den, Grizzly gave a sharp, piercing whistle. This brought her erect once again, facing him. At this instant he fired right at her heart, dropped his rifle, and drew his pistol and bowie knife. The burly female staggered backward as the ball struck her breast. She began to paw and bite at the ground. To Adams, this was a sure sign of a fatal shot and he rushed upon her, bowie knife poised. She looked dead enough to him, with blood gushing from her chest and dying her coat crimson. He discharged all six chambers of his revolver into the huge form and at least one of the shots took effect right under her left ear. But, just to be sure, he reached down to slit her throat. When the knife blade touched her, however, she revived and leaped up to clutch Adams in her muscular paws!

"I had not much time to think, for it was obviously a death struggle for one or both of us and as her horrible teeth met in my flesh, the exquisite pain left me nothing but an instinctive sense of the necessity for prompt action. We were both down upon the ground together, now. Her teeth and claws were both at work. I was desperately struggling to get my arms free for offensive measures but, growing exhausted with my loss of blood, I was not at first successful. At length, I twisted myself around underneath her and, catching her with my left hand by the great goatee which hung under her mouth, I plunged my knife into her heart with my right and worked it briskly round to insure its fatal operation. Her jaws opened, her claws relaxed their hold; and after one or two more spasmodic endeavors to mutilate me, she rolled over and expired."

The hunter, who shortly before had been so anxious to attack, feeling, in his own words, "steady as a piece of ordnance upon a battery," was wobbly and woozy. He was mangled, even crippled, and desperately weak from loss of blood. All around him, the grass was stained with gore—much of it his own. (Nevertheless he boasted, later, of that weak-kneed moment, "But I was worth twenty dead men, yet.") Only a slowly circling buzzard was witness to the death struggle. "I was alone in the gorge," he recalled, "and as I looked upon the dead monster I felt like Alexander, sated with victory and wishing another foe worthy of my prowess to engage."

Adams bound up his wounds and lay down on the grass to rest. After some time, he summoned up his strength and hauled himself to his feet. With drawn bowie knife, he began to creep into the cave. It was pitch-dark in the cavern so

Adams, fearing the male might still be within, prudently withdrew. Outside, he collected pine branches, fat with pitch, and using them for torches, he re-entered the lair and explored it by the blazing light of the faggots. Even as gritty a fellow as the Wild Yankee had his weaker moments and this was one of them. Later he confessed, "My heart panted quite as much with alarm as with interest. I will acknowledge it, I was really full of fear. I was a long distance underground. I had no assistance to expect. I was miles away from the camp and intruding upon the very premises of the enemy."

But he had his reloaded rifle and pistol and keen knife. His courage was coming back along with his strength. On and on he crept into the bowels of the mountain on his lacerated knees. The glare of his fuming torch finally showed him a chamber almost five feet high. Its floor was littered with leaves and grass, and in a nest there he found two beautiful little cubs, hardly a week old, their eyes not yet open, and no bigger than wharf rats. Taking them from their leafy beds, he examined them and found them to be healthy, lively males. He looked about for a third cub, since he knew that a grizzly's litter was often three young, but no other babe was to be found. Taking them up by the nape of the neck again, he plopped them inside his buckskin hunting jacket, between that garment and his woolen shirt, where they would be warm and safe.

"Scrambling out of the cave, no king upon his throne could have felt prouder than I did," Adams recalled that moment. He literally danced and capered for joy over his exploit and his prizes, as he made his way to the place where he had tethered his mule, Betz. The animal was not there. At first, Adams thought it had been stolen by Indians. But, glancing skyward, he saw that his bag of dried venison remained undisturbed in the tree. Circling the spot, he soon came upon panther tracks and realized that one of the big cats had attacked his mount and caused the mule to break away.

Grizzly settled down to tracking the mule through the chaparral and, after passing over a single hill and down a cañon,
he found the animal grazing placidly in a grassy valley. The
mule started with fright as he approached but his call of
"Betz! Betz!" soon reassured it and the mule came up to
him, glad to see its master again. On its haunches were deep,
bloody scratches, evidence that the cougar had leaped upon
its back.

Adams mounted up and returned to the dead grizzly. He
butchered the animal, packed a portion of the meat and left
the remainder just inside the mouth of the den, then proceeded toward camp whistling and humming and singing in
the best of spirits although his frame was bruised and bloody.
Back at camp, his white companion and the Indians laughed
at his wild tale, declaring it pure invention—for all his scars
and cicatrices—until he popped his hand into his jacket front
and pulled out the two cubs, like a magician. Placing them
before Saxon/Solon, he let him choose one for himself,
although the hunter protested that he had not earned it. But
Adams insisted on their arrangement of share and share alike,
for which he received many thanks from his companion.

The men went on talking until the dying embers signaled
the lateness of the hour. Just before they turned in, Adams's
companion named his pet—General Jackson. Always ready
to have the last word, Adams remarked that General Jackson
was, indeed, a great man but that he knew of a much greater
man and that he would name his cub after that gentleman—
Ben Franklin.

The next morning, after his companion indicated that he
would like to see the grizzly's lair, Adams led a hunt in that
direction. From the bloody battlefield he led the way into
the cave. Adams was annoyed, if not surprised, to find that
his cache of meat was already torn to shreds and almost devoured. He blamed the watchful "vultures"—the turkey
buzzards. But Adams was wrong, as he soon found out. He

suggested that his friend lead the way with one of the pine torches he now lit, but Saxon declined. Adams took the torch back from him and dropped to his knees to enter the den. To his astonishment, he heard leaves rustling in the supposedly empty cave. This did not stop Adams, who was still thinking of a possible third cub. But next a low, unmistakable, warning growl echoed in the chamber and Grizzly stopped dead in his tracks. Holding the torch over his head and the pistol at the ready, he peered into the shadows. Suddenly his glance was answered by the piercing, malevolent eyes of a wolf, sitting on its haunches and grinning ferociously at him.

A coward with his back to the wall can be a dangerous adversary, and Adams did not discount the wolf's desperation. "Many men in this situation would have been very willing to let him alone, but I determined to give him fight," recalled Adams. Calling to his companion to back him up, if necessary, Adams jabbed the butt of the torch into the ground and took his bowie knife in his left hand. The pistol in his right hand spat fire into the gloom just as the trapped beast, with a growl, sprang for the entrance of the cave. There was no time for a second shot. The first one did not take effect and the beast bounded past Adams, almost atop him. But he was able to grab the wolf by its bushy tail. This did not stop it, or hardly slow it up, but it gave Adams time to strike it once with his knife and Saxon/Solon gave it a blow with a club which stretched it out, cold and dead.

Sure now that the den was finally clear of danger, Adams, in his annoying fashion, could not help teasing Saxon some more. Stooping down and crawling in, he halted after only a few feet and cried out, theatrically, "Beware of the other wolf!" His companion, just then entering, scuttled back out to daylight in a fright which tickled Adams no end. He saw that his friend was moving from fright to anger at him but was able to laugh the wrath out of him. Grudgingly, Saxon entered the cave, finally, and explored it with Grizzly.

Back at camp, the Old Yankee found a problem on his hands—raising the cubs. There was no milch cow about camp, of course, so the hunter cast about for a substitute for mother's milk. He tried a mixture of water, flour and sugar which was hardly a howling success. Luckily, the problem was solved by Adams's greyhound bitch. The dog had just had a litter of pups. Grizzly got rid of all of them but one and turned the two cubs over to the greyhound. At first, the dog was snappy with such bizarre and ugly foster children but eventually she accepted them and let them suckle. Before long, she was licking and lapping their coats and playing with the runty cubs as if they were her own puppies. They grew so fast—especially their claws—that Adams had to make buckskin mittens for them to spare the greyhound a scratching when they fed. After four or five weeks of this, he got them to eat pounded meat and, finally, was able to wean them entirely.

Adams continued his hunting while his companion took loads of fresh or dried meat down to the mines, for a neat profit. On one trip, Grizzly went down, taking Tuolumne with him and, instead of a pack mule, Lady Washington, bearing a packsaddle like the Mexican *aparejo,* but of green hide. With this, she cheerfully would carry 200 pounds of meat.

Another time, Adams took Lady Washington on an overnight hunt. Camping in a wild area of caves and boulders, cliffs and shelves, cedars and pines, they were approached by a gray wolf and two pups, beset with curiosity. Adams easily killed the mother but had trouble capturing the pups, which ran into a cleft in a rock. However, he smoked them out. One he caught by the scruff of the neck but the other he had to grasp by the tail and this fellow twisted about and sank its fangs into Adams's hand. The stubborn Adams did not let go, however; he had the determination of a snapping turtle. He kept his hold and tied them both up. As he and the tame grizzly lazed about the fire, Adams saw half a dozen pairs of eyes glisten in the shadows. It was a beautiful sight and he was almost sorry when his rifle shot brought down a deer and put the rest of the band to flight. Sleep was hard to come by that night, for wolves and mountain lions circled the lonely camp, howling and screaming.

When dawn finally broke in the east, Adams got up and mounted the high cliffs above his camp. In a rocky and barren region, much higher up in the Sierra than he would usually go for good hunting, he spied a flock of the very timid mountain sheep. He crept within twenty yards of the bighorns but could only get a bead on a poor animal, an old ram with one of its horns broken. There was no chance of getting a better trophy, so he fired. The ram bounded in the air—"like a piece of India-rubber"—and fell dead. The rest of the flock scampered up into inaccessible cliffs and ledges. Before he could even reload, there was not an animal still in view. Grizzly packed the ram and the deer on Lady Washington and, putting the wolf pups in a sack, headed back to camp.

Tradition has it that the mountain lion will never attack an adult human. Adams learned differently. On a hunt with Solon/Saxon, he separated from his companion. He had gone a quarter of a mile when he heard his friend cry out for help. Bounding up the hill to the ridge which separated them, Adams looked into the ravine below to see his comrade, flat on the ground, with a puma apparently gnawing at his neck! Shouting to his friend to lie as still as death, Adams fired. For fear of hitting his friend, he shot wide but the panther took fright and bounded off, its long tail flying behind it.

A very shaken Saxon (or Solon) explained the curious incident. He had been walking up the creek, looking forward and paying not the slightest attention to the trees overhead. Suddenly the beast dropped from a limb, right on top of him, dug in its claws and set to work with its teeth and jaws. Saxon/Solon had only time to cry out for help and to pull the hood of his buckskin coat over his neck. This probably saved his life. Adams, while he appreciated his friend's forethought, could not understand why he had not, instead, reached for his knife to stab the animal. So he asked, "Why didn't you fight the panther?"

His companion replied, "I was afraid to move, supposing it would only infuriate the animal."

Adams's ornery streak showed itself, as it so often did, and he chided him: "Such a caution would have been good in the case of a bear, but a panther is made of different stuff. By nature a coward and sneak, he has the cruelty of cowardice, daring combat only when he has the sure advantage and wreaking a bloodthirsty ferocity most upon an unresisting victim. A determined stroke of the knife," advised Grizzly, "would have terrified him and put him to flight."

Done with his excoriation of his companion, he stripped off the latter's coat and found his back severely scratched and his neck bitten, but not severely, thanks to the buckskin. Adams used his perennial water cure, moving his patient to a spring where he poured water on the wounds through a tube of bark until Saxon/Solon complained of the cold. Then Grizzly soaked his friend's shirt in the spring and over that put both his own coat and his friend's. He also prescribed water internally, insisting that his wounded companion drink and drink, although he was not thirsty. Adams said that it would induce perspiration, which always eased pain. His docile patient followed his directions and, warming up and perspiring, just as Dr. Adams had predicted, he said he felt better when he arrived in camp. There, however, a more careful examination by Grizzly revealed that he had two deep bites where his neck joined the back of his head. It was necessary for the hirsute surgeon, who never used a razor, of course, to shave the nape of his companion's neck with his bowie knife. As a barber, Adams had considerably less skill than as a general practitioner, and his victim wailed and howled during the tonsorial operation, cursing him and shouting that he was worse than the panther. He absolutely refused to let Adams hack away anymore but the hunter just signaled to Tuolumne, who grabbed hold of the "customer's" head and Grizzly trimmed away until the hair was as short as the nap on a piece of velvet. Then he cleaned the gashes, bandaged them with wet rags, and put his patient to bed.

Next day, Adams attended to the mountain lion. He took Tuolumne and headed for the ravine where it had attacked his hunting companion. They soon found its trail and tracked it into a brushy cañon where they had to creep and crawl, pushing aside thorny chaparral branches all the while. They were startled by a low growl into caution and looking into a crevice in some rocks they saw the puma glaring at them. Blood spatters on the trail had already told Adams that his shot of the day before had not been as wide as he had thought. Now, he noticed blood on the puma's coat and even on the five kittens which crowded up against her.

Grizzly gave Tuolumne the sign to fire first, thinking to himself: "He is a good marksman. If he kills, it will be a great encouragement to him. If he does not, it will require a degree of coolness which he does not possess to fire an effective second shot." The ball struck the great cat but did not kill. However, as the animal turned to flee, exposing one of its sides, Adams fired and dropped the cougar in its tracks. The two captured the tiny kittens, only a week or so old, then skinned the dead animal, keeping the claws and head intact, as well as the pelt. Examining the carcass, Adams found that his shot of the day before had struck the animal at the junction of shoulder and neck.

When they arrived at camp, their patient complained so

loudly of loneliness that the Yankee presented him with the puma pelt to cheer him up. While he mended, Adams and Tuolumne went out on expeditions to try to bag some big-horns, but even as good a hunter as Grizzly Adams was thwarted by their vigilance and their keen sense of smell. He was not successful for all his scrambling about precipices and pinnacles.

A few days later, the men broke camp and returned to their Merced River campsite. Besides many bales of dried meat and hides they had the makings of a real menagerie in the two grizzly cubs, two wolf pups, two fawns, and five pan-ther kittens. The hunter loaded the wild animals, suitably encased in boxes or baskets, on the mules and Lady Wash-ington. All went well until the kittens, on the bear, began a dolorous whining which upset the grizzly. However, when Adams led her along the trail she became quiet again.

To pay Stanislaus, who had protected their camp so well during their absence, Adams presented him with a brand-new bowie knife, a new suit of buckskins and some blankets which Saxon or Solon had bought on one of his trips down to the mining settlements. He did the same for Tuolumne, for his hunting help. Both boys assured him that they were eager to rejoin him in a mid-spring, 1854, expedition to the Rocky Mountains.

CHAPTER VIII

TRANS-SIERRA TRAILS

APRIL 1854 was half spent before Grizzly Adams was ready to set out for the Rockies. He had already busied himself for several weeks in preparing for the long trek. His plan was to hunt not only for specimens and trophies but for meat, to boot. As market hunters, he and his new companion, Gray, a miner and ex-Mississippian from Chinese Camp, could earn good money by selling game to emigrants on the Overland Trail. Adams felt that it would be a longer and probably more dangerous tour of duty than his trip to Kennasket's area. He was heading for the land of the almost legendary grizzlies of Lewis and Clark, not to mention the often hostile Indians of the Rockies and the adjacent High Plains. Thus, before he left, he sold some of his animals and otherwise settled his accounts though, in truth (according to Adams), he was more the creditor than the debtor. However, he had long since given up any idea of collecting so much as a plugged rupee of all the money due him.

He went down to Howard's Ranch and left all of his animals save a yoke of oxen, two mules, Lady Washington, Ben Franklin and the cub's foster brother, the greyhound pup, Rambler. Grizzly liked the look of his new partner, Gray, who, in fact, resembled him not a little. The Southerner was young and hardy but, like Adams, wore a full beard and moustache and a long, untamed head of hair. "He was an excellent hunter," appraised Adams, "and a trustworthy friend." Gray was to get one-third of the profits and Adams, as leader, organizer and provider of a wagon, oxen and mules, the other two-thirds. Gray planned to return to his home state from the Rockies and carried on his person a thousand dollars in gold dust to realize that aim.

Once the snow was burned off the lower mountain slopes, Adams gave the order to move out. He consented when about twenty-five Indians asked to be allowed to go over the mountains with him, to fish in the lakes on the eastern side of the Sierra Nevada. At first, he had considered Indians to be miserable subhumans, though he always was ready to help them in their precarious struggle for existence by killing a deer for them. But as the beauty and solitude of the Sierra began to leech the bitter misanthropy from his soul, Adams found feelings of humanity overcoming him. In a way, the Indians would be responsible for his eventual reconciliation with civilized man, a few years later. In 1860 he admitted as much: "Even these people, I convinced myself, Providence had created for a purpose which, I doubted not, they fulfilled; and I soon could not help reflecting that, whatever of evil or good there was in the world, and whether they did me harm or advantage, it was the part of philosophy and wisdom to take them as they were and make the best of them. This, indeed, is the great and I may say, the fundamental, lesson of life; and it was thus and there, in the mountains, that I successfully worked out for myself the great problem which other men have to work out, each in his own way, before they can say that they live."

Yoking the oxen, he hitched the mules before them to pull the wagon, and chained Lady Washington to the rear axletree. Ben and Rambler, because of their youth, were allowed to ride in the wagon bed. But the greyhound bitch and Chief Kennasket's mutt ran loose. The throng of Diggers followed the vehicle at a respectable distance. Adams led the way, with Gray and the strutting Indians, Tuolumne and Stanislaus, proud as peacocks with their new possessions (just given them by Adams)—Colt revolvers and crimson scarves. The sun, rising, limned the caravan against the dense screen of pines and firs and, hours later, when sinking, threw a last wash of rosy light on the cavalcade as it came to a halt in the snow near the headwaters of the Tuolumne's Middle Fork. All in all, though the so-called Emigrant Trail was hardly a track, it had been a beautiful day and Adams's party had made good progress that first march. Before bedding down, however, Adams warned his Indian allies that the next day would be the first of many difficult ones of snow and steep ascents. He gave them a deer which Gray had killed, urged them to be faithful to him, and then heard out their assurances of loyalty.

The crust of the four- to five-foot-deep snow on the mountain which blocked their way began to thaw as the sun rose next day but Adams's usual early start got the caravan over the worst of it in good style, although he had to call on the Indians to haul the wagon over the summit with ropes. The ridge was the farthest point which Adams had reached in that direction, before. He was faced with a difficult decision since he had no guide and the snow was much deeper than he had expected so late in the season. All he could do was to order his men to push on eastward over mountain after mountain. At one point, the Indians had to go to work with the two pickaxes, three shovels, three axes and many sharpened stakes to dig a road in the side of a vast snowbank. It was so steep that he ordered them to trench out a rut, or track, for the inside wheels to ride in, for safety's sake. Men and squaws alike worked hard on Adams's promise of a big dinner. Six years later, Grizzly Adams would brag of his success: "Being myself something of a teamster, I yelled at my animals with great success upon this occasion, and helped them up the hill as effectively as ever the best driver in the world could have done."

At the pass, he drew his little crew up in a circle to splice the mainbrace. From his old leather *bota*, he poured drink after drink of Sonora's best brandy into the tin cups thrust toward him. Behind him trailed Tuolumne with water for chasers, and Stanislaus brought up the rear with a bag of sugar. Adams gave a drink to all hands—braves, squaws and papooses—but just enough to put everyone in good spirits without intoxicating them. When he was through, less than two pints remained in the leather bottle but he knew that a quart of his fine, high-proof *aguardiente* was worth half a gallon of the rotgut dispensed in Mother Lode saloons. He vowed, looking toward heaven (or so he claimed) that the rest would not be touched, except as medicine. At camptime, Adams had his Indian followers dig out a large circle in the snow under a big pine, then bring in all the firewood they could find. Meanwhile, Adams and Gray cut up several dry pine logs to add to the kindling of sticks and boughs which the Indians gleaned. The result was a roaring fire, probably the biggest that the redskins had ever enjoyed, since they ("improvident creatures!") customarily built tiny fires to huddle about. The ravenous company cleaned up every scrap of the roast venison served them; then Adams gave them dessert by tossing a half-dozen plugs of chewing tobacco to the braves.

Although it was very cold at the high altitude of their camp, it was a clear, moon-washed night and the dark sky's fabric was soon rent and torn by jagged, blazing stars. It was no effort for Adams to get his allies to dance in such splendid weather, and the jogging, singing and whooping went on till very late, when he finally ordered them to their blankets. They all rolled themselves into one tangled mass, for warmth. Giving them a last order, not to move around during the night, he posted Gray as a guard and rolled up in his blankets.

But the chorusing cries of wolves, coyotes and mountain lions, attracted by the smell of cooking venison, denied him sleep and he eventually arose to join Gray on post, taking Tuolumne with him.

A daring pack of wolves, toward dawn, made an assault on the camp. Tuolumne and Adams fired on them and they turned tail and fled. When daylight came, Adams found a wolf with its back broken by one of the shots. He quickly put the *lobo* out of its misery with a slash of his skinning knife. Next, the excited dogs lit out on the trail of a panther and soon treed the big cat. Gray and Adams fired as one man. Gray's ball hit the puma in the heart; Grizzly's drilled into its head. The cat dropped to the ground and the two men took it by the hind legs and dragged the carcass to camp, throwing it into the wagon for possible use as provisions. After breakfast, Adams had Tuolumne and Stanislaus melt snow to water the animals, then gave the order to break camp.

Up a narrow cañon they climbed, till the walls closed in on the company so tightly that the wagon could not pass. Adams realized that he had missed the "road" of the emigrants. There was no room to turn around; retreat was impossible. So Adams had the Indians take down the vehicle and lug the parts on till the pass opened up again. Melting snow further slowed their progress but after much pulling, tugging and portaging of luggage, to lighten the wagon, they reached firmer snow near the summit of the white-blanketed cordillera.

Supper included roasted mountain-lion meat which tasted good to the fatigued men. There was neither dancing nor singing that night; all hands turned in quickly. Before dawn, a new start was made. But progress was slow and when Adams examined the hands of some of the complaining Indian workers, he was surprised to find them blistered. But he encouraged those in good shape with a promise that this was the last day of hard work of muscling the wagon over the

Sierra. Soon, all of the Indians had blistered hands and Grizzly had to shift much of the baggage to muleback, returning later with the mules to pull the empty wagon.

It was dark when the topmost ridge was reached but only a mile or two of a downhill run brought them to a site on the steep eastern slope which provided firewood. When they camped, it was with a feeling of triumph over nature and all were in good spirits. Grizzly Adams himself was elated and, with his usual immodesty, trumpeted in his memoirs; "I claim no great credit for leading my army over the California Alps, but perhaps my difficulties were, in proportion, as great as ever were those of Hannibal or Napoleon. . . . Had I fallen upon the valleys at the eastern base of the Sierra with carnage and blood, I, too, might have garnered a niche in the temple of fame, and my passage of the snowy mountains might have lived in story. But my mission was a peaceful and an humble one, and what I accomplished was the work of my own hands."

Dawn revealed a scene of great grandeur and beauty. From the summit, Gray and Grizzly watched the sun rise into a cloudless sky over the Washoe deserts. North and south stretched the jagged saw blade of the Sierra Nevada's summit, softened with a blanket of snow turned crimson by the low rays of the sun. It was so glorious a sight that both men watched the changing colors for a full hour though they had to stamp about and slap their arms against their sides to fight the cold. They spent the whole day running and sliding down the slope, braking the wagon which, even with chain-locked wheels, moved like a juggernaut.

At an abandoned log cabin built by Sonora traders the company found a veritable junkyard of wheels, axletrees and wagons, some broken and some in good condition. Gray suggested that they adopt one of the lightest wagons but Adams vetoed the idea, reminding his friend that the vehicles, still, were the property of emigrants who had had to abandon them like shipwrecks.

Over hill and dale, in and out of cañons and arroyos, the party continued on, leaving behind the snow although the timber stayed with them. In the foothills they found new green grass springing up through the dried stalks of the previous year, so they turned their animals out to graze. Adams gave the order to lay over for a day of hunting, to restore their depleted larder which was reduced to a bag of flour, half a bag of *pinole* (Indian meal), fifty pounds of dried meat, and a little sugar and coffee, for thirty wandering and hungry souls.

Gray, sizing up the country east of the Sierra—drier and more barren than any he had seen—was a dour prophet. He predicted failure in the hunt. Not so, said the more experienced Californian. The country, to him, had all the signs of a great wild game preserve. Mustering his army, he set out to prove his contention. He had twelve Indians, armed with bows and arrows, besides his own men. Putting Tuolumne in charge of six of them, with a mule, he sent his squad in a northeast direction. Stanislaus he sent with four more men and a mule in a southeast course while he took the remaining pair, and Lady Washington. He took a bearing on some hills lying almost due east and set out toward them. Gray held the fort at camp, with several Indian oldsters, the squaws and children, to help oversee the animals.

Grizzly's party came upon a herd of fifteen to twenty antelope in a few miles. Tying the Lady to a tree, he ordered his men to make a surround. As they set about this, Adams moved directly toward a knoll among the scrub oaks and junipers. From there he saw one of his Indians decoying the antelope by waving his cap on the end of a stick, back and forth. The antelope were pointing like hunting dogs, hypnotized by the slowly swaying cap. When the animals had approached to within eight to ten yards of him, the Indian laid down his decoy, drew his bow and buried an arrow to the feathers in the side of one antelope. As he remained still and

hidden, the others of the band did not panic but remained
and he was able to let drive two more arrows. Now Adams
fired. The band turned and looked at him. As they did so,
Grizzly slowly raised the red Mexican sash he had taken
from his waist, to do a little decoying himself. As they advanced, propelled by their deadly curiosity, Adams reloaded
and fired, bringing down a buck. Finally, they sped away as
fast as the wind. Only one carcass lay on the ground but three
more were wounded and Adams and one of his Indians soon
killed two of them. The third escaped after a long pursuit.
After dining on antelope steaks, they packed the meat on
Lady Washington and headed back for camp, meeting, en
route, the other Indian, who had bagged an eagle, some
crows and several jackrabbits.

At camp, Adams found that Tuolumne had brought in a
brown bear, many hares and a mess of magpies, crows, hawks
and grouse. The bear had given him some tense moments.
His first shot failed to bring the beast down and four of his
men fled. However, four stood by him and shot the beast
full of arrows while Tuolumne reloaded and finished the
bear off. Adams ordered a big fire laid, a feast spread and two
dance rings prepared by the Indians. He fired his rifle as a
signal and was pleased when Stanislaus responded from the
hills to the southeast by discharging his own weapon. When
Stanislaus brought his party in, their mule was laden with
two deer and a mixed bag of birds and hares. After dinner,
the Indians kicked up their heels in a dance to celebrate their
successful hunt. The dance, which lasted late into the evening, so infected Gray with its rhythm that he took part,
showing the redskins a Southern hoedown. Adams could not
tolerate being upstaged, of course, so he participated for a
few moments with Yankee dances he had learned in boyhood. "But my gray head and long white beard ill comported
with the lightness of my heels," he ruefully admitted, "and
the Indians, particularly the squaws, almost burst with

laughter at the figure I made. So, I resumed my seat and my old pipe, fully satisfied that my dancing days were over."

Two days more brought the company to the Walker River, where the Indians planned to leave Adams. They were bound down the river to Walker Lake to fish, while Grizzly meant to strike straight across the desert from the Walker to the Carson River. There was almost no timber now, except on the very banks of the river, only sage and greasewood. In fact, there was hardly any wood for fires except for the litter of driftwood on the banks of the Walker itself. Game thinned out, too, save for squirrels and prairie dogs. The river, where they struck it, was wide and deep with snowmelt. It was lined with cottonwoods, ash and alder. The trees were black with buzzards which took off in welcome and soared and darted down at the camp, hungry for its meat. One giant bird was particularly aggressive, as if he were the King of the Vultures. It was, in fact, a California condor. Adams fired at the great bird and broke one of its wings. When he approached the wounded condor, now flopping on the ground, the huge bird made such a show of ferocity that he decided to give its powerful beak a wide berth. He had Tuolumne put a pistol ball into its head.

The atmosphere here played tricks with the men, too. Once, Adams was astonished to see an immense animal ahead. It appeared to be bigger than a buffalo and Adams began to wonder if it were not an elephant and, if so, what it was doing in the Nevada desert. Coming close, a mirage dissolved and the hunter found it to be just a normal-sized horse which had probably escaped from an emigrant train. (A few days later, he built a brush corral and trapped the horse, to add to his remuda.)

While camped on the banks of the Walker, Gray, on guard duty one night, awoke Grizzly to report the sound of footsteps in the dark near camp. The Mississippian feared an attack by Indians and asked if he should not put out the fire.

Grizzly told him not to do so because the Indians could see far better in the dark than whites. Then Adams listened intently, rifle in hand. Shortly, he relaxed and smiled, telling Gray that the noises were made by animals, not redskins. "Now, if I am right," he added, "a whistle will tell the tale." He pursed his lips and gave a sharp blast between his teeth. It was answered immediately by the unmistakable snort of a bear. Adams moved back from the stump where the game was piled, to let the bear approach closer. When the beast ventured into the firelight, after the meat, he and Gray rose up, fired and bored it through the gut. Now the camp was plunged into chaos, for the Indians awoke and came up, jabbering, to see what was going on. The bear suddenly revived and, to the redskins' consternation, rushed into their midst. In the confusion, the bear pinned one brave and bit him badly in the thigh. Gray and Adams rushed in to strike the beast with their knives and saved the man but not before Adams himself received a bad bite in the left arm.

CHAPTER IX

PANTHERS AND SAINTS

RAFTING across the unfordable Walker on cottonwood logs, Adams led his party over a forty-mile desert to the Carson River. Their water bags were soon dry and the two-day march was made unpleasant by acute thirst. But they reached the Carson safely enough. There were no trees on its bank and the men were unable to make campfires. It was a damp and foggy camp that night, but they were rewarded with good grass for the animals. Proceeding downriver, catching trout with grasshoppers as bait, and killing beaver to vary their diet, they took off from the great bend toward the Humboldt Mountains in the middle of what would become the state of Nevada. Grizzly had heard much of this range from forty-niners. They had told him strange tales of even stranger animals—black and white wolves and purple panthers!

Again fashioning a raft of cottonwood boles, the men crossed the Carson and set out across the desert, a *terra incognita*. A faint thickness of the eastward horizon Adams took to be the far-off line of the Humboldt Range, sixty or eighty miles ahead. For three days they pushed on over barren country, the mountains plainly in sight in the clear morning air but retreating into indistinctness during the hazy-smoky afternoons. At last the wanderers struck a beautiful little stream which wasted its sparkling waters in a desert sink out in the Great Basin. They followed it up to the Humboldt chain, which they found to be a wall-like barrier. Adams skirted along the base of the range for fifteen miles, seeking a pass or some kind of break. At last, a rugged cañon opened up, hardly wide enough to admit the wagon. Following the little brook in its bottom, and crossing and recrossing it a dozen times, they reached a little grassy valley enclosed by hills covered with pines and cedars. This Adams chose as his headquarters for a week of hunting before pushing on to the Rocky Mountains.

A reconnaissance of the Humboldts was hardly promising. The mountains were barren and rocky; any timber was thin and scrubby. The men killed some grouse, jackrabbits and squirrels but only a few deer, and did not even see bears, must less panthers either purple or otherwise hued. But finally Adams found a rugged, brushy mountain full of ledges, clefts and caverns. In this paradise for panthers they soon found fresh tracks of cougars. The two Indians who had joined Adams at the Walker proved to be good trackers and they soon brought him to a cliff with caves and crevices, below which were the bones of many kills. Grizzly ordered fires kindled to smoke the big catamounts out but the wind changed and the fires, instead, smoked the hunters out. Taking pine torches, Adams and Gray then entered several caves but found nothing so they bedded down to keep a night watch on the panther village.

After night fell, the cañon soon began to ring with the shrieks of pumas. The cats could be heard crashing in the brush, too, but not a one was seen. Finally, an Indian reported to Adams that he had found a den occupied by young ones. It was steep country and Adams and the Indian had to let themselves down a cliff from one small handhold to another. They found themselves in a rubbish heap of bones —"a perfect Golgotha of the animal kingdom," Adams called it. There were hair and feathers and the bones of antelope, deer, wolves and coyotes scattered everywhere. Some were crisp and white, others yellowed with age. Grizzly figured that the den had been occupied by predators since the days of Methuselah.

About sundown, Adams, Gray, and the two Indians took up their vigil some fifty yards from the den's mouth. Soon, two cougars, one male and one female, came gamboling down the cañon. They were met by three kittens which came out of the den to play with their parents like house cats. Giving Gray the signal, a whistle, Adams fired and brought down the female. Gray fired, too, but also at the female, and the male was unhurt. But, though startled by the explosions, it did not yet see the men and rather than running off, pranced about, screeching. Adams fired after a quick reloading but only wounded his target. The cat made a great spring toward Gray. Adams thought it was attacking his friend and, shouting loudly, he ran to his aid with his bowie knife drawn. But the long-tailed puma was only frightened and bounded right past the men to disappear into the brush. They never saw it again.

The kittens scurried back into their cave after dodging effectively the efforts of Adams and Gray to trap them under their buckskin coats. Adams lit a torch and prepared to enter the den but, at first, Gray balked. Grizzly reminded him that the adults were disposed of so there could be very little chance of danger. His friend replied, like a man, that he would share any danger, anyway. Adams wrapped his coat around his neck and, as Gray followed suit, he put a little cayenne pepper in his pocket. (This he often carried, along with snuff, to blind opponents at close quarters, if necessary.) His left hand held both a torch and his knife; his right bore his cocked revolver. Creeping and crunching their way over the skeletons and loose bones littering the cave floor, the two men entered a second and third chamber. In the last, the little catamounts raised up, bristling and spitting. Adams and Gray laid aside their weapons and loosed their coats. Adams dashed pepper into the faces of the little lions, then both sprang on them with coats spread out like nets. In a few moments, they were free of the stuffy and smoky cave. They exited to find a mob of worried Indians awaiting them. The acoustics of the cave had been so strange that they enlarged every sound within and the onlookers hardly knew what was coming out.

Finally, an exultant Adams had time to give a close look to the dead cougar. But, for the life of him, he could see nothing purplish about the panther. It was as tawny as the sand on which it lay and looked no different from any other catamount he had killed.

The day after Adams and Gray stormed the lion's den, one of the Indians found a wolf's lair, with whelps playing in front of it. The hunters found it to be a tunnel-like opening in a hillside, probably the home of a bear taken over by the *lobos* when bruin vacated it. After a patient watch failed to pay off, Adams let his men try to dig the pups out. The men had no tools with them and, working with only pointed sticks, progress was very slow. But three hours of labor produced a shaft some five to six feet deep into the hill, which broke into an inner chamber of the den. The "room" was three or four feet in diameter and carpeted with leaves and hair. Adams led a meticulous examination of the den but found no wolves. Fresh spoor led him to deduce that it had just been abandoned. He figured that the old wolf had discovered the Indian at the same time that the Indian found the den. In any case, it had vamoosed. Twenty-four hours of patient watching and hard digging resulted in nothing but aching muscles.

Scouring the Humboldt Range for provisions, the men were discouraged to find nothing alive in the savage and barren country. By nighttime, the hunters were all suffering from thirst and hunger. But one of the Indians suddenly whispered to Adams, "There's a bear!" It was true. Adams studied the beast rooting along the side of a ravine and concluded that there would be water in the gulch, too. Things began to look brighter. Gray stationed himself in a clump of bushes, then shot and wounded the bear. Adams finished it off. Never was a ham roasted faster than on that occasion, for the men were almost starving. After satisfying their thirst, the men spread out their bedrolls and dropped into a sound sleep.

When their hunting, next day, took them near the panther's cave, Adams decided to revisit it, using torches. With his men, he removed some loose stones inside and found several other chambers. These he and Gray explored until Gray caught sight of a glimmer of light ahead. Putting their torches behind them, they both could see, plainly, daylight ahead only eight or ten yards. They groped their way into what seemed to be a different den from the one they had entered. Both wished that they had not left their rifles at the mouth of the first cave. (Six years later, Adams would write, "It inspires in me more dread now than, when under the excitement of the hunt, I crept into it.") The hair at the nape of his neck prickled as Gray cried out, "A panther!" As yet, Adams saw nothing but he plainly heard the low growl of a wild thing. Then he saw it, a large puma with flaming eyes. His first thought was to retreat but this would have been madness. To turn their backs would invite attack. So Adams advanced with Gray right behind him. There was not enough room to proceed side by side. Nor did the catamount seek to retreat; it angrily growled and glowered at the men. Expecting a sudden spring, Adams pointed his Colt right at the gleaming eyes and fired. The blast of the pistol was followed by a tremendous, echoing screech but the two hunters pressed on, firing and yelling as they progressed. The terrified animal rushed for the opening and vanished.

Adams asked Gray to go back in to collect the cubs, but the Southerner suggested that they both return for the kittens. No, said Adams, the dam might return. (He did not believe this for a moment but he wanted to test Gray's courage as he had Saxey's, Tuolumne's and Stanislaus's, in the past.) So, with blazing pine knot in one hand and knife in the other, Adams crawled back into the gloomy recess. Placing the five cubs inside his coat he crept back to the entrance. There, where Gray could see him, he put the Southerner to the test. Grimacing in mock horror, Adams shouted, "Help me! Help me! For God's sake!"

Gray rushed up to him, crying, "What's the matter?"

Adams shrieked a panic-stricken reply, "The panther! The panther! Pull me out! Pull me out!" At the same time, he writhed and twisted as if a catamount had him by the legs.

Gray unhesitatingly grabbed him by the arms and pulled him from the cave whereupon, to the Mississippian's astonishment, the Old Yankee leaped to his feet, laughing, to slap him on the back and praise him for redeeming himself after his early timidity, or cowardice.

The soft but clear air of the desert mountains just east of the Humboldt Sink was pleasant, if not exhilarating, and even Adams began to laze about camp rather than go hunting. He brought all the animals together and had them frolicking in happy play, making friends out of such natural enemies as dogs, bears, wolves and mountain lions. He particularly fostered the growing friendship between Rambler, the greyhound pup, and Ben Franklin, the young grizzly, since he wanted both to be his future hunting companions. The result was a Damon and Pythias-like alliance of the foster brothers.

Glancing up from the chaotic circus in the meadow, Adams was surprised to see clouds piling up like great snowbanks atop the mountains. The higher they piled, the darker they became. Even a fool could see that a storm was making up and Adams lost little time in making the camp secure. But no one was prepared for the speed of the tempest which rolled over them. The men had barely time to roll their rifles in their blankets and pile large logs on the fire when the black heavens opened up and spewed wind-driven hail-stones on them like grapeshot. A whirlwind was driving the hail and as soon as he saw the twister, Adams ordered his men away from the wagon under which they were taking shelter. Instead, he ordered them to lie flat on the ground in their blankets. The cyclone hit the camp, picked up the wagon and whirled it around, throwing baggage to all points of the compass. Trees, too, were thrashed and twisted, and some were uprooted. The storm was brief but all the men were bruised by the hail barrage as well as soaked to the skin. The sky cleared and the men rekindled the fire but again the sky darkened and a second tornado struck the camp with drenching rains, lightning and a drum roll of thunder. ("Frightful! Terrific! Never in my life, before or after, have I seen anything so appalling," recalled Adams.) Fortunately, the wagon was spared, thanks to Adams's quick thinking in loading it with boulders during the lull. The men crept out of their hiding places in the brush with the animals, tried to dry themselves and their baggage, more than ready to take the next leg of the journey to the Rockies—Meriwether Lewis's "Shining Mountains."

To be ready for the long desert road to the Salt Lake country, Grizzly sent all hands out on hunts to build up his store of rations. Five deer fell to their guns, then a bear, and nine antelope, plus foxes and wolves enough to turn the camp into a jerky and buckskin and fur factory. The last chore was greasing the wagon's wheels with bear fat and speculating, around a last night's campfire, over the hazards of the desert march ahead.

Early the next morning, the expeditionaries, man and beast, moved out. Ben Franklin was now old enough and strong enough to travel on foot. Adams did not even chain him, as he did Lady Washington, but let him range freely. Running out of the foothills, they camped at a water hole where they filled all their containers for the dry stretch ahead. Most of their march lay over a parched, sandy waste. The dreary landscape became volcanic, dark, a burnt *malpais,* then glaring alkali flats and dry soda lakes. Forty miles they marched and still found no trace of the spring which mountain man Joe Walker had described to Adams. Camp that night was a dry one, without water, fuel or grass. Suffering acutely from thirst, the men pushed on with Adams far ahead on scout. Luck rode with him; he found water in a group of mounds. But they were twenty miles ahead of the caravan and Gray predicted the draft animals would never reach the water. However, as evening cooled the air, the animals revived somewhat and Adams, sending his men and beasts ahead, took command of the wagon to alternately coax and bully his team slowly to the filthy, brackish, but life-saving spring by morning.

Two days were spent at the mounds, because of the presence of a little grass with the alkaline water. On the next segment of the trek, the supply of water gave out entirely again. No emigrant had traveled the route and Adams realized that he had strayed off the course Joseph R. Walker had told him to take. He lamented that Walker, "though perfectly truthful, was difficult to understand." When his party stopped for the night, Adams did not rest with them but rode off to reconnoiter ahead and to the sides of his route of march. Ten miles distant, he found a spring. It took the exhausted animals all day to stagger their way to the water.

Ben Franklin's feet were now cut and sore and tortured by the hot sand. At first, Adams put the bear back in the wagon but Ben liked to run and play so much that the hunter tried to keep him at liberty. He therefore made moccasins for his pet, of elkskin soles and buckskin uppers, sewed with thongs. He bound them so tightly to the grizzly's feet that Ben could not bite or tear them off. They remained intact for several weeks, long enough for Ben's feet to heal.

The day before Adams's party reached Utah Lake, Grizzly encountered six horsemen driving a few loaded mules. These were the first white men they had seen since leaving California. Neither party wished to delay long in the desert but the men chatted for a few minutes and Adams learned that the strangers had wintered at Salt Lake City and were on their way to the Pacific Coast.

The next evening brought the Californians to Utah Lake. Adams found it an immense body of water, locked in a thick belt of tules. Its surface was thick with ducks and geese. The next day, striking southwestward, they became mired in crossing a small, muddy stream and had to uncouple the wagon to pull it out, piecemeal. But the foul black mud was cut with the tracks of elk. This sign delighted Adams; it meant that the lean days were over. After crossing several sloughs, the men built a raft to cross a more formidable stream and moved into handsome country, grassy and dotted with trees. Everywhere was the sign of deer, antelope, elk, bear and even buffalo.

To replenish his depleted stores, Adams ordered his men out on a buffalo hunt to the east. Finding a small herd, the men managed to kill two though they found their horses so jaded that the buffalo easily outran them. While they were cutting up their game, Adams saw a small party of well-armed Indians approaching. They were unsuccessful hunters and they asked Grizzly for something to eat. No novice at prairie politics, Adams gave them their fill and they went off happily, praising the white men as their true brothers. At camp that night, Adams's men, for their own part, enjoyed their first good meal since leaving the refuge of the Humboldt Mountains.

Deer, elk, antelope and foxes, as well as buffalo, fell to the huntsmen. Proceeding onward, keeping now to a northward course, Adams's men fell in with several white hunters who told them they were about seventy miles from the Overland Trail and Salt Lake City. As they rode toward the Emigrant Road, Gray scouted ahead. He soon came hurrying back, chortling, "If you want to fight a Rocky Mountain grizzly bear, I can take you to one in a few minutes." However, he added, "It would be foolish to go after him, since our team is already loaded down."

Adams snorted, "It would be foolish to allow the first Rocky Mountain grizzly we have met to escape!"

With Tuolumne tailing him, Adams poked into a bushy ravine and spied his first Rocky Mountain grizzly. He was disappointed. The animal, about which he had heard so much, looked small in comparison with the denizens of the Sierra Nevada. However, the many tales of the Rocky Mountain critter's ferocity led Adams to treat it with care. He crept up on the beast, busy stuffing itself with berries, and gave it a sharp whistle, such as would have brought a California bear to attention. The shrill noise had no effect whatsoever on bruin. Next, Adams tried an outlandish yell. This, at least, caused the bear to look up, sniff—and then return to its berrying. This imperturbability began to worry the hunter. As Adams later confessed, "The reputation of the beast made me feel nervous and it was some time before I could steady my aim; indeed before firing I was extraordinarily careful to see that my pistol and knife were ready for a close encounter, and that a tree was nearby for refuge." But when he fired, he bored the beast right through the heart and before its groans had ceased, he had reloaded and planted a second bullet under one of its ears. Just to make sure of the beast, he slit its throat, then gave it a careful once-over. He guessed that it would weight about 500 pounds. The bear had light-colored eyes and light, long, coarse hair —almost white. No wonder Meriwether Lewis had termed them "white bears" as well as grizzled bears. Taking the hide and some of the meat, the two men continued on to rejoin the others and make their way to the point where the Emigrant Trail crossed Muddy Fork, there to camp.

Before beginning his collecting and meat hunting for the emigrants, Adams decided to pay a visit to the fabled City of the Saints, only fifty or sixty miles distant. He timed his trip so that he could spend his favorite holiday, the Fourth of July, in the Mormon capital.

Two and a half days of travel brought Adams and his companions to the heart of Deseret. Along the road they sold meat to overlanders and when the trekkers were too poor to pay, he gave them food as well as entertainment in the form of his cavorting panthers, fawns and wolves, two-by-two (Noah's ark style). In the city, he sold his hides and the young wild animals for excellent prices, then spent the rest of July 3, 1854, touring the wide streets and squares. The next day, there was a celebration and speech at what Adams took to be the Temple (it must have been the Tabernacle). While no close friend of Mormonism, Adams was more objective than most of his Gentile peers and less hostile to the Saints. In 1860 he wrote, "I thought then, as I think now, that it does no good to listen to what the Mormons have to say, but it may do much to look at what they have done, and what they are doing. It has been usual to call these singular people fanatics, and I can see no harm in giving them their proper names; but when it is considered that all the world is more or less fanatical, and that it is the privilege of only a few to deserve the name of true liberality, I can hardly look upon the Mormons with what is generally considered orthodox contempt. There must be something good, among the much evil, to keep them together, and their wonderful labors in their Rocky Mountain city attest the fact that there is, at least, earnestness and vigor in their counsels. They are equal to the Jews of old in their hatred of the Gentiles; but it seems to me that their entire organization and polity is much more of a political than of a religious character."

If he was, perhaps, a little ambivalent in the case of Mormonism, Adams had no qualifications in his opinion of the head of the Latter-day Saints. He did not cotton to Brigham Young. He heard him preach and then described him: "He was a great, fat, pursy, individual—just such a worthy person as an alderman is always described to me—a sort of human compound of fish, flesh, fowl and other good things generally. He seemed to know a good deal about Heaven, but it was the Heaven which he represented in himself. He was Heaven all over, he seemed to intimate; and all who wanted to go to Heaven had only to go to him. He spoke as if he and his Maker were on very intimate terms, indeed, and had no secrets from each other, and he threatened all who did not yield him complete obedience with the vengeance of the Deity, just as if he had it under lock and key and could dispose of it by special license to suit his own purpose. I never heard such blasphemous bombast in my life before, and am sure I shall never want to hear anything like it again!"

Later, Adams was able to pay the saintly windbag of his recollection a rather backhanded compliment. He had heard a good deal about the local Screeching Bears, so-called from their noisy habits. When he finally was able to lasso one, *Californio*-style, and drag it back to his camp, his prisoner gave vent to such a screeching that Adams named it Brigham Young, on the spot.

Upon his return from civilization, Grizzly led a series of buffalo hunts out from his camp. On their first hunt, he and his men were able to drive a large herd up a ravine in the side of a mountain. The result was like shooting carp in a Japanese pond, though they only killed three. Dressing out the meat, Adams sent Gray and one of the Indians with it to the Emigrant Trail to sell or trade it. The remainder Adams packed to camp on Lady Washington, now almost as tractable with Tuolumne as with Grizzly himself. She proved to be worth as much to them as a horse or mule in the hunt.

A week more the Californians spent in hunting buffalo and trading, working their way up to, and past, Fort Bridger. He used the surround instead of stalking, the method he normally employed on other game. Compared with grizzly bear hunting, it was pretty tame and one hunt seemed like every other one. But some hunts were exceptional, such as the one on the day when he led a half-dozen whites and five Indians in a surround of a gang of between 200 and 300 bison. Again he managed to drive them into a steep ravine. Although the animals stampeded in an attempt to break the circle of men pouring rifle fire in on them, more than twenty-five finally lay stretched on the ground, to be sold. All of the men were kept busy that day skinning out and butchering the buffalo for the California-bound emigrants. Next day, they hauled the buffalo beef up to the trading post (Fort Bridger?) and, after it was sold, Adams divided up the handsome profits—twenty-five cents a pound—in shares. Although Lady Washington got no pay, she too seemed to enjoy the hunt and willingly carried up to 300 pounds of meat for short distances and occasionally let Adams ride her. However, he never really expected to employ her in that manner except in emergencies.

During this season, Adams and his men tried lassoing buffalo and were successful in snaring five calves. One of them lived to star in Adams's menagerie on Broadway, New York. (The other one sent east fell sick on shipboard and died on the passage around Cape Horn.) When the market for buffalo beef grew slow, Adams moved his operations up past Fort Bridger to the area of Ham's Fork, between the trail to Salt Lake and the bend of Bear River. Here they hunted and traded again for a week, during which time Tuolumne had a close brush with death in a grizzly hunt. The Indian and Adams found the beast emerging from a wallow, covered with mud. He came toward them, lying down from time to time to roll in the grass and remove the mud clinging to his thick coat. Finally, he stopped and sniffed the air. Adams waited no longer. He fired and hit the grizzly right in the snout. Tuolumne then stepped out into the open, drew a bead on the beast and fired. But on came the bear. The Indian dropped his gun and sprang into a pine tree. The bear stopped to sniff the oily, metallic rifle, poking at it with a paw, so Tuolumne fired six pistol balls into the beast. This had little effect except that the grizzly reared up on its haunches. This action gave Adams a clear shot with his re-loaded rifle. But even this rifle ball, which sped straight to the animal's heart, did not do it in. The tenacious animal ran back 300 yards to the pool in which it had been wallow-ing, then fell dead. When Adams examined the carcass, he found that the pistol balls had failed to penetrate the layers of fat under the shaggy coat. After dining on fresh bear meat, the two were accosted by a second grizzly. Again, Adams let Tuolumne have the first shot. This time, the bear ran off, lickety-split, something which, thought Adams, no California grizzly worthy of the name would have done. In sizing up the two bruin brothers, Adams came to feel that the Rocky Mountain creature was a little overrated: "The Rocky Moun-tain beast is not always so ready to fight. He is more danger-ous than the Calilfornia grizzly in his disposition to follow up a trail, but in a fight, though terrible enough, he is not to be feared like his cousin of the Sierra."

Bored with the routine of buffalo hunting, and with plenty of money in his pockets for the first time in many a moon, Adams decided to devote the last part of his stay to grizzly hunting although in the haziness of his recollection a few years later, he thought he had gone as far east as the Platte after buffalo. Assuming that he remembered correctly, and did reach the famous river "too thick to drink and too thin to plow," he may have killed some Rocky Mountain sheep, as he also claimed, driving them from the very riverbank to the open plains where there was no cover, and harrying the animals to exhaustion. He said that he and the two Indian youths captured two animals with their reatas, one of which he later exhibited in his San Francisco menagerie. (The other died of some disorder.) The mountain sheep, unfortunately, became a playmate of Ben Franklin, who accidentally hugged the ram to death. Adams saved the fine head of the sheep and took it to New York with him to exhibit, when he left San Francisco.

Adams came close to not surviving that last hunt in the Rockies. He learned a lesson, the hardest way: never underestimate a grizzly—even a non-California b'ar! It was a beautiful day to take a grizzly, he mused. He and the Indian boys moved up to a deep ravine clothed with thick chaparral and trees. In it they found fresh bear tracks and, tying up the horses, they crawled through the bushes until they came upon an oldish she-bear playing with two cubs in a pool of water. Adams did not want to break up the charming scene of romping and cuffing but when the adult animal began to leave the water hole, he remembered that he was a hunter and he snapped off a shot. The ball did not go true. He aimed at the heart but it hit her in shoulder or paunch. She rushed at him like a runaway express train, giving him no time to reload, to run, even to dodge. He did reverse his rifle and, grasping the barrel, swung it like a club. The blow on the beast's head did not faze her, but it gave Adams time enough to jump into the creek, and draw his knife. She was atop him in a moment, bearing him to the ground in her crushing hug. She shifted a paw to his head and, pinning him down as helpless as a mounted butterfly, she bit him deeply in the shoulder. Adams never forgot that moment, almost his last

on earth, even if he forgot whether he had apprehended one
or both of the cubs by that time or not. (In one account, he
claimed that a cub was crushed to death inside his hunting
jacket by the hugging grizzly.) "The next instant, she had
thrown me upon the earth, face downwards. As she planted
her teeth in me, I turned and, taking my old and favorite
hold with bears, I caught her by the goatee with one hand
and my knife felt its way to her bosom with the other. She
bit me severely in the back, arms and legs but while she was
lacerating my limbs, my weapon was letting out her lifeblood
and she soon fell over, dead."

The bloody braggart now had to lash out at his companions
for cowardice, as he seemed compelled to do after every close
shave. Perhaps egged on by the pain of throbbing wounds, he
shouted to his companions, who had disappeared into the
buckbrush. "Gray! Gray!" he called. Then, muttering, "The
cowards have left me."

But Gray answered, "Hello!"

Adams shouted back, "Where are you?"

"I'm here," the man replied, from a hundred yards away.

"Do you expect to help me there?" snarled Grizzly Adams.
"Come and catch these cubs. I've dispatched the bear."

To Adams's exasperation, Gray asked, "Is she dead?"

Angrily, Grizzly roared, "Yes, she is dead, but it was no
coward that killed her!"

Gray was grumbling an insult in return but when he came
up, commiserated, "Adams, I thought you were gone this
time."

Grizzly was now beside himself. "It is only cowards," he
shouted, "who are *gone* in the hour of danger! You have acted
in this affair like a miserable coyote!"

Adams brusquely ordered Gray and Stanislaus to catch
the cub or cubs. (One, if Adams's Recollection No. 2 of the
struggle was correct; two if he did not have one inside his
shirt while wrestling with the mother bear.) Impatiently, he

took a hand when he saw the men were too slow to catch the nimble little creatures. "You are more clumsy than cowardly! See the Old Hunter catch them!" Whipping off his cap, he used it like a net to snare the cubs. "See there!" he shouted in self-satisfaction, holding up a cub by the ears though his wounds hurt him terribly.

When his cuts and bites healed, Adams was right back on the trail of Rocky Mountain grizzlies. His last real hunt before heading back for California was climaxed when he came upon a grizzly feeding on the carcass of a buffalo in the rugged country near Smith's Fork of Bear River. He fired for the heart but the animal neither dropped, fled nor rushed at him. Instead, it wheeled, snapping at its tail like a mad dog. Though astonished, Adams had the presence of mind to reload and fire again. Gray and Tuolumne also shot the animal. When it finally expired, he found that his first bullet had hit in its spine and caused the strange reflex. Adams guessed that the damage to the animal's spinal cord had caused what would have been called insanity in a human.

Shortly after this encounter, Gray told Adams that he was going to break up the partnership and head for the South. He planned to join some men going east from the nearby trading post. So Adams split up the property and settled Gray's account. Always grudging in praise (except for himself), Adams nevertheless thought pretty well of the Mississippian, saying, "He was a good hunter but, like most hunters, not overfond of grizzly bears."

When they parted, Adams took Ben and the Lady, two bears, two deer, two wolves, some foxes, many skins and two panthers, which died shortly. He also had about a thousand dollars in cash which, for safekeeping, he hid in the bed of the wagon, digging out a hiding place with auger and chisel. When interrupted in this work by a passerby, who said he would weaken the wagon, he lamely answered that he wanted a mortise so he could raise a mast and hoist sail to catch a breeze. Apparently none of these emigrants had ever seen a wind wagon and they went away shaking their heads over the mad mountain man who was wrecking his vehicle in an obvious fit.

Adams led his two California Indians back toward their homeland via Fort Hall and Lewis's Fork, picking up three horses, six cows and two oxen, all abandoned by overlanders. These recruits to his ambling menagerie made travel slow and it was nearly the end of September, with packs of snow on the peaks, when he reached the east face of the Sierra Nevada.

CHAPTER X

RETURN TO THE RANGE OF LIGHT

BEFORE attempting to cross the High Sierra, Adams decided to camp for a few days to recruit his party's strength. The men had seen no bears since leaving the Rockies but once they were in the California cordillera again, they were visited by prowling grizzlies, one of which came right up to the camp and poleaxed a cow with a blow of one great paw. Adams struck right back, surprising the white-haired raider by starlight. After his whistle arrested the beast, still tearing at the dead cow, the marksman planted a ball in its heart and quickly followed this up with a knife stroke to the same organ. The Yankee was knocked over by the beast's death throes but escaped unhurt as the Indian boys rushed to his aid. The three cut up the grizzly and later tried out fifteen gallons of oil from its fat.

After a five-day rest, Grizzly yoked up his animals for the steep pull over the summit to his home on the west slope. The soft snow made for sloppy going but hard work kept the wheels rolling and, only a few days later, the company was running pell-mell downhill through increasingly familiar scenes. However, some of the vistas were strange to Adams. He found that many of the wild areas which he had known in the Sierra were being tamed, with squatters camping everywhere. One once-familiar grassy flat, for instance, he found to be turned into a great earthen dam and reservoir for mining purposes. A worse blow was in store for him. When he reached his old homestead on the upper Tuolumne River in October, Adams found nothing but a heap of ashes. The fire which had overrun his old campsite had spared nothing but the tools which he had prudently (as ever) cached in a cave.

But, thanks to his helpers, Adams soon had a new, snug cabin and stable erected to ward off winter's cold. When everything was shipshape, including three new traps to replace those burned up, Adams told Tuolumne and Stanislaus that they could leave for the winter season. But they did not choose to go down to the foothills, as yet, although Adams gave them a horse apiece, a new set of buckskins and $100, enough to transform them into nabobs among their tribesmen.

Letters reached Grizzly Adams at this time from his brother "William," * informing him of a contract which the latter had made to send two large grizzlies and one small bear to Lima, Peru. Grizzly answered, by letter, that he already had one large and one small bear at Howard's Ranch, and that he was sure that he would be able to provide another in a few weeks. In fact, it was only a few nights later that one of his new traps caught a grizzly. Adams immediately wrote to his brother that he would deliver the animals to Stockton at a certain date, either to him or to his agent.

Adams then built a cage for the new bear while Tuolumne went down to Howard's Ranch for a team. A few days later, the hunter set out, driving the wagon with the caged bear. At Howard's he hired a teamster and outfit to haul the other two bears and they left for Stockton together. Their trip was uneventful until they were on the outskirts of the San Joa-

---

* The best genealogical records available on the Adams families of New England suggest that Adams had no brother named William, although he had eight siblings.

quin River port. There they were accosted by a do-gooding blacksmith who told Adams that he had no business bringing bears into the city. "We are not going to have any more bear fights in *this* city!" he thundered. After Adams learned from the smith that a man named Dunbar had just been killed by a bear a few days before, he calmly reminded the man of the story of another of his breed, Demetrius of Ephesus, cautioned him against "the dangers of uproar," and entered Stockton.

A large crowd gathered around the colorful, hirsute figure in buckskins, following him and his bears all the way to the steamboat landing where he would place them aboard ship for San Francisco and, eventually, Lima. Some of the more sadistic or dim-witted of the onlookers tormented the captive creatures by poking them with sticks. Grizzly, naturally, shed no tears when one of them brought a buttock within striking distance. The hunter described the result, delicately: "One individual, happening to get too close to one of the cages, suddenly lost a pawful of meat; the want of which probably interferes with his comfort, while sitting, to this day." The badly scraped fellow drew his pistol, intending to seek revenge, but Adams pulled out his own revolver and reminded the angry miner that the bear had only acted in simple self-defense. He also advised him that he was standing by his grizzly to the death. The Yankee outtalked and outbluffed the pistol-wielding, cursing miner and, as a result, won a cheer from the curious crowd. "Hurrah for the Wild Yankee!" they shouted. When the wounded fellow saw the temper of his fellow citizens, he suddenly withdrew. The crowd of men remained, however, till the animals were all safely aboard ship. Adams felt obliged to treat them all to drinks.

Back in the mountains once again, Adams loafed about for a few days until his blood grew stagnant (as he put it), then decided to seek once more a truly colossal grizzly of which the Indians had told him much. He had hunted the animal unsuccessfully the winter before, but, this time, he wanted to take the giant grizzly alive. In his wide-ranging hunts for the animal at this time, Adams may have visited Yosemite again. In any case, somewhere near Yosemite Valley, he finally came upon a fresh trail of the great bear and he followed it to the hidden den. "His home was in a deep cañon," Adams later remembered, "and not very tempting for exploration. It was amid a dark and dismal-looking collection of the wildest scenery, overgrown in all directions by almost impenetrable bush, and full of chaparral."

Giving long and hard thought to the problem of taking the huge grizzly alive, Adams finally decided to build a trap hut, or heavy-duty box trap, on a hill nearby, which he saw that the bear frequented. For ten days, Adams and his Indian boys, using the span of mules for the heaviest work, slaved over the log trap. They first dug two parallel ditches, about six feet apart, and then laid a fourteen-foot pine log in each. To these, he attached cross timbers, each one about a foot in diameter, for a strong foundation. Next, he set horizontal side timbers, twelve feet long, locking them in place with cross timbers at the ends. A picket of six-foot perpendicular timbers finished the skeletal log house which he anchored to a tree on one side and to a deep-driven stake on the other. Lastly, Adams split logs to make puncheons and, with these, built a strong door, facing the smooth side inward. He suspended it from a long lever which was tripped by a sort of trigger to which the bait was attached inside the pen.

When all was ready, Adams baited the trap with a freshly killed deer, removed all wood chips, covered the area around the huge trap with dirt and leaves to kill the human scent, and settled down to wait. It was now November and he was ready to wait all winter if he had to. Many times, from his hiding place, he spied the behemoth those next few days. It was the biggest grizzly Adams had ever seen. ("He looked like a moving mountain and my heart fluttered for fear of being discovered.") He later estimated that he had had fifty chances to shoot the beast but he had held his fire, determined to take the giant alive. Regularly, he checked his big trap but the grizzly was wary. During an unbroken four-day close watch, for example, the mountaineer saw the bear several times go as far as the trapdoor to sniff the bait but some bearish sixth sense always told him not to enter. In desperation, Adams took to dragging bloody bait over hill and dale before dumping it into the trap. This did not work, although he killed fifteen deer and a number of coyotes and rabbits for bait during the wearying period. He even tried strewing a trail of sugar into the pen, knowing the love felt by grizzlies for the sweet granules. But this sacrifice of his coffee sweetening failed, too.

The mountain man was almost ready to give up when, one cold night, he was awakened from his sleep by a great noise. "It was the awfullest roaring and echoing in the mountains I ever hear, with the single exception of the appalling thunderstorm in the Humboldt Mountains." Adams thought to himself, "It is either The Bear or Old Nick, himself, and I guess it's not the latter." Jumping to his feet, he ran outside where the thunder of rage convinced him that he had his prey at last. He called to a delighted Tuolumne and the two set out over the snow, its surface frozen to a hard crust by the cold snap. They reached the trap, a mile and a half away from their camp, and, lifting their blazing pine-knot torches, saw the grizzly caught in the trap but making such violent lunges at them that they feared he would shake the stout cage to pieces. The men built a fire and settled down, occasionally strengthening the trap by the addition of more timbers. For more than a week, Adams stood guard over the trapped giant while Tuolumne brought him food and water by day, and, now and again, camped overnight with him to keep him company.

For an entire week, the animal raged and fought against his captivity, biting and gnawing at the logs with his teeth and tearing at them with his long claws, setting the whole structure to shaking. At these moments of high rage, Adams tried to tame him by beating him with a crowbar and throwing firebrands into the pen. Only when the animal tired and fell asleep did Adams allow himself to curl up in his blankets to rest. On the eight and ninth days, the bear's wild spirit—as well as his strength—appeared to be weakening. Adams realized that the battle was won when he detected these signs of surrender. "When this species of subjugation takes place, there is no further trouble with a bear until he is removed to a new cage; and then the same process, though usually not so severe, has to be gone through." By teasing the bear unmercifully, Adams had not only tired him but had successfully diverted his powerful claws and fangs from their task of reducing the trap to kindling. Still the strength of the giant was so great that Adams admiringly dubbed him Samson. And he did not let him out of the trap for literally weeks, feeling that it would be too dangerous to try to move him.

While Adams was away from the trapped behemoth, he hired four woodcutters, whom he found chopping out timber for a mining flume, to take care of the bear and to water and feed him. It was more than a month after Samson's capture that Old Adams finally felt that the time was ripe to cage him and to haul him to his semipermanent camp. (He had already shifted from his old Tuolumne River homestead, when winter snows made game scarce, to a better camp on the Merced, below Yosemite.) During his absence from his vicious new pet, Adams had dropped down out of the mountains, "in a fine fever of delight." He went to Howard's Ranch, as usual, and there hired a *ranchero* named Combe to be his helper. He sent Combe to join Tuolumne and Stanislaus while he visited Hornitos and Stockton.

He wanted Tuolumne to accompany him to civilization

but the Indian balked, saying, "Bad people at Hornitos." Grizzly did not know what kind of a scrape the boy had gotten into among the rough gentry of that Mexican mining town and he could not pry it out of the lad, so he went alone. He genuinely liked and respected the two Diggers and, five years later, mused, "In recalling their good qualities to mind, I cannot but remark that, in comparing ourselves with the Indians, we are all too apt to disregard the centuries of slow advancement which have removed us from the savage state. We are apt to look upon the roaming tribes as an inferior race but the inference is unauthorized and unjust."

On his way back to the mountains, Grizzly hired S. E. Hollister and a teamster with a yoke of oxen, to help cage the grizzled monster and haul him to Stockton. (In a few years, Hollister would ape Adams and become a pretty expert bear hunter, though not in Grizzly's class, and would be the subject of an exciting lithograph of the 1860's showing him, "The Great American Hunter," stabbing a grizzly to death somewhere between the American and Cosumnes rivers.)

By the time Adams was finally ready to transfer Samson from his much-gnawed prison to the iron cage which the Old Yankee had bought in Sonora, two full months had elapsed since the grizzly's entrapment. But, although he had fallen off a little in flesh, or fat, he seemed to have lost little of his strength or temper and it took the efforts of all of the men to effect the transfer. The men were tired before they even began to tug and haul at the bear, for the road to the trap was agonizingly slow and difficult. To get the cumbersome wagon, weighed down with the heavy cage, up to the trapped bear, they had to cut a swath through the timber and, for the last fifteen miles, literally dig out a road to allow the ox-drawn vehicle to pass.

The Old Hunter had his men bring the iron cage up tightly against the entrance of the trap. He hoisted both doors and patiently waited. But nothing happened. The obstinate beast did not choose to emigrate, even a few feet, although the men whipped his flanks to drive him out of the trap. Samson was used to his pen; it was, apparently, far preferable as a home to the strange contraption with the stink of metal all over it. Once again, Adams had recourse to the firebrands. They failed. He even tried to lever the monster out, by prying at his bulk with a crowbar. It was hopeless. So, Adams sent his exhausted crew to camp to rest while he perched up on top of the cage, ready to drop the door should the bear venture in. He might just as well have rolled up in his blankets for a good night's sleep. Samson refused to budge.

The clear, sharp, night air helped Adams's thinking and, next morning, he was busy trying to lasso the beast with a log chain, letting it down through the cracks between the logs. In vain he tried, time after time, to work it around Samson's legs or neck with long hooks. It took the whole day but at 4 o'clock he finally snared the grizzly with a loop of his chain. Adams managed to pass the end of the logging chain out the door of the trap, into the cage, and out through its back bars. He then turned it over to the teamster, who hitched his yoke of oxen to it and goaded them forward. Although Adams prodded Samson with an iron rod and the oxen pulled like the powerful dumb brutes they were, the grizzly braced himself against the door and could not be dislodged. Once more, Adams leaped to the attack, in the bear's rear, with blazing brands. The combination of these tormenting torches and the straining muscles of the oxen prevailed. Samson was wrenched loose and dragged ignominiously into his new home. There he immediately bounded to his feet again, mad with rage. But Adams had given the quick order to the teamster atop the cage, who dropped the door shut with a metallic clank that spelled *finis* to Samson's hope of ever escaping.

So violent was the grizzly's frenzy that Adams stayed at the cage all that night, using his rod of iron and his blazing brands in attempts to curb his captive's wild rage. Next day, the Yankee had his helpers remove the wheels on one side of the wagon. Somehow, they managed to boost the cage up the inclined wagon bed, like a sawlog being loaded, and, righting the vehicle, they replaced the wheels. In a few hours, the men had broken camp and were on their way, via Howard's Ranch, for a brand-new camp Adams had selected, far from the Sierra. It lay in Corral Hollow, in the heart of California's Coast Range lion and grizzly country.

CHAPTER XI

CORRAL HOLLOW

SAMSON proved to be such a load for the wagon that Grizzly made very slow progress, taking three days just to reach Howard's Ranch, where he left the giant bear and his other pets, except for Lady Washington, Ben and Rambler, for the summer. Adams had heard much of the lion country around Corral Hollow in the lee of gloomy Mount Diablo. And if the catamounts were not to be encountered in the Hollow, it was near Livermore's Pass (now Altamont Pass) where pumas were sure to be found. Breaking his new camp on the Merced, Adams and Combe set out for Mount Diablo. In three days or so of travel they hit the San Francisco–San Joaquin road where it debouched out of the Coast Range via Corral Hollow (Arroyo Buenos Aires), a ten- or twelve-mile gash in the steep hills sprawling away from rugged Diablo. Through it, in winter, a stream roared. In summer, it usually dwindled to a dry arroyo or lost its slight flow in the flats before reaching the San Joaquin.

Adams stopped at an inn and saloon kept by two men, one named Wright and the other Edward Carroll, on the Corral Hollow road. He struck a bargain with the first man, who abandoned his publican's duties for the season to serve as Adams's helper. The three men—Adams, Combe and Wright —set to building three traps, which, once they were finished, they placed in the wildest, roughest and most desolate of the cañons of that lonely region. They also hunted deer with success, and sold the venison to travelers on the road. Traffic was heavy that summer for San Franciscans, many of whom had westered to the city as the Mother Lode petered out and were now heading east to the San Joaquin Valley to make their way down its entire length to the Kern River mines, recently discovered. They usually took Livermore's Pass or Corral Hollow to reach the river before making southing toward the Tehachapi Mountains and the Kern.

Although he did not lack courage entirely, Combe showed very little talent as a nimrod. Adams customarily left him in charge of the camp and the animals (the chores for which he had hired him, after all) and either hunted alone or with Wright. Wright was a better hunter and companion in the field than Combe. He was, in fact, a quite good deer hunter. But, as Adams wrote later, "Like all other men who have had little experience, he was dreadfully afraid of a grizzly bear."

Corral Hollow had little of the look of either bear or lion country. Adams found the whole Diablo Range of the coastal mountains to be in marked contrast to the timbered High Sierra. Most of the high hills and low mountains were bald as eagle eggs. It was bone-dry country in summer, but he found a spring and a handful of oaks, for shade, about three miles downstream from the big bend where the coal mines (later, the ghost town of Tesla) were located. His camp was two cañons west of the later ghost brickyard town, Carnegie.

Even today, the hot, dry and often treeless Diablo Range is little explored and little known. It is less familiar than the High Sierra to most Californians. Small wonder, then, that it was good lion and bear country in Adams's day. A half-dozen years after he left there, Geological Surveyor William H. Brewer described the general area: "Back of the treeless hills that lie along the San Joaquin plain there rises a labyrinth of ridges, furrowed and separated by deep canyons. These ridges rise 3,200 to 4,000 feet high, with scattered trees over them, sometimes, but not often, with some chaparral. This region is twenty-five to thirty miles wide and extends far to the southeast—I know not how far, but perhaps two hundred miles. It is almost a *terra incognita*. No map represents it, no explorers touch it; a few hunters know something of it, and all unite in giving it a hard name. Two different ones, one a companion of old Grizzly Adams, have described it as 'a hell of a country,' and, so far as our observations go, they were not far from correct." What did Brewer think of Yankee Adams's old Hollow, itself? "We find it a most Godforsaken, cheerless, inhospitable, comfortless region. . . . Much of the region around here is practically a desert; not called so, but really so. The bed of this stream [Corral Hollow Creek] tells of a large stream at times but often years pass without any water flowing down it to the plain, much less to the [San Joaquin] River beyond."

It was in October 1861 and June 1862 that Brewer visited Corral Hollow. The first year, he actually camped at what was called Adams's Spring, for Grizzly, near the ruins of the Yankee's old cabin. Here he bought a deer from a onetime hunting companion of Adams's, perhaps Combe or Wright. Although he was fairly comfortable in Adams's oasis and enjoyed the geological wonders of the area, Brewer did not like the lonely Hollow and was glad to leave after a week in 1861.

The rough country did not faze the Old Yankee, however, in the least. He was able to thrive in the most inhospitable *malpais*. In one of the steepest, rocky and brush-filled of cañons, named Devil's Den, Adams discovered both a bed of coal and a mineral spring. He was just about to call them to his companion's attention when he was interrupted by the snort of a grizzly bear, close. Too close! Adams looked up, to find himself confronted by two curious yearling cubs and their powerful mother. The big bear was up on her hind legs, ready to offer battle. Poor Wright! He took one look at the beast and demonstrated of what metal he was made. Trembling like an aspen leaf, he cried out the one word—"Run!" —then took his own advice. Adams was left to face the bear, alone.

Years later, Grizzly remembered that moment when Wright panicked and left him alone with *Ursus horribilis.* "I knew very well there was no use running, under the circumstances, nor, indeed, did I feel any disposition to do so. For it was seldom that I ever let a bear escape me and it was pretty evident on this occasion, in particular, that if I did not kill her, she would kill me. As there was nothing to be hoped for from Wright, I paid no attention to where he went. But, giving my whole attention to the bear, I watched my opportunity as she came snorting towards me and planted a ball fairly in her heart. As she received it, she fell over backwards and never rose afterwards."

Immediately reloading, while keeping his eye on the fallen bear, Adams shouted to Wright, "Why don't you shoot the cubs?" His companion pleaded that they were bobbing about so much that he could not get a good aim at them. But Wright's voice was quavering with nervousness and when Adams finally saw him, Wright was perched on top of a high rock, up which he had madly scrambled in his flight. He was pointing his rifle at the two cubs nosing and yelping around their mother's inert body but so wobbly was his aim that the gunsight traced little circles in the air. Sarcastically, Adams called to him, "When you do get aim, shoot!" By now, Adams was reloaded so he took aim and laid one of the two cubs low with a ball at the base of its ear. Wright now took courage and fired but the ball did not hit within twenty yards (said Adams) of the cub. "Wright always pretended that he did not really shoot at it, but I questioned it then, and I doubt it now. He was too much scared to shoot anything."

Once again, Adams reloaded but the surviving cub charged at him. There was no great danger from such a yearling, other than a bad scratching, but he dropped his still-useless rifle to draw his knife. Meeting the cub halfway in its rush, he caught it by the long hair of its underjaw, with his left hand, as it reared up, and struck with the knife in his right fist. The blade plunged into the young bear's abdomen, to the hilt. Adams yanked it out and sunk it again, this time behind the animal's foreshoulder, where it reached the heart. The cub dropped and died at his feet, having given him but one sharp blow, on the thigh.

The Old Yankee turned to see where his companion was now. To his disgust, Wright was still sitting on his rock. He had not even attempted to reload after his wild shot.

"Are they dead, Adams?" he asked.

"No, you had better stay there till they stop kicking," snorted the Yankee.

"Well," said Wright, "I thought they would kill you, surely, and I saved my life while I could."

While he cut the throats of the three bears, as insurance against accident, Adams observed to his shaking comrade, "That's a comfortable doctrine, but your bones, too, would have whitened this valley, if they had killed me. You are a good climber, I see. But when you talk of running up rocks, look at these claws."

Leaving the carcasses where they lay, Wright and Adams returned to camp to find Combe with a party of visitors. They were Argonauts, bound for the Kern River. After Adams told them of the hunt, a half-dozen volunteered to help him pack the bear meat into camp. Some of them refused to believe that Adams, single-handed, had dispatched three grizzlies with two shots and two stabs, in as many minutes. However, their disbelief changed to amazement and admiration when their inspection of the carcasses testified to Adams's great hunting prowess.

A few days later, other visitors came to Grizzly Adams's camp. They were three hunters from the redwoods country on the peninsula south of San Francisco. They told Adams that they had heard much of his hunting skill and said that they would be much obliged if he would allow them to join him in the field for a few days. Adams was agreeable, and took them on a hunt. They encountered a she-bear and cub. Directing the redwoods men to take care of the young one, the Yank stretched the mother out, dead. All three of his new companions fired at once and the cub dropped and lay still. However, when Adams examined the animal he found that there was but one wound in the body. He showed this to the men and an argument immediately broke out among them, each one claiming that his shot had hit the mark while the others had missed entirely. "Each one gave so many reasons why he could not have missed," Adams recalled, "that I amused myself for a long time laughing at them." At last, they appealed to the Wild Yankee to settle the controversy. He did so in Solomonic style, deciding that all three shots had struck at exactly the same spot, making but one visible bullet hole. Thus, they were all entitled to credit for the kill.

Shortly after the hunt with the redwood country men, Adams was delighted by the birth of a cub to Lady Washington. The little ball of fur thrived and Adams named him Fremont. After the birth of the young'un, Adams took a little vacation, of sorts. He paid a visit to his old Sierra hangout. Already he was thinking of removing to San Francisco, or some city, to show his menagerie of animals for pay. He had a hunch that he could make a living at it. But first, he wanted one last look at his Sierran hunting grounds. As fate would have it, this spring of 1855 expedition came near being his *last* trip anywhere. He drove the wagon, taking only Ben

Franklin and the dog, Rambler, leaving both Combe and Wright in camp in Corral Hollow.

On his way into camp from a fatiguing hunt, Adams was leisurely cutting his way through a *bosque* of chaparral when he heard a stick break close to him, almost at his very side. His blood ran cold when he saw that a huge, silent grizzly, trailed by three cubs, was flexing her muscles to spring at him. There was no time to shoot or even to avoid the beast's spring. Adams tried to raise his rifle, mostly by reflex action, but it was smashed from his grasp by a great sweeping blow of a paw which sent him reeling to the ground. Dizzied, Adams awaited the fangs and claws which were now his due. But, as his head unfogged and he could clear his eyes again, he saw that both the greyhound, Rambler, and his pet grizzly, Ben Franklin, had rushed to his relief. The dog seized the dam by one thigh while young Ben went right at her throat. They worried the big female enough to distract her from her chore of tearing at Adams. The fallen Yankee needed nothing more than those few moments of grace. Springing to his feet, he grabbed up his rifle and aimed it just as the wild beast bit Ben Franklin horribly about the head and neck. Uttering a wild shout, which caused the mother bear to rear up, Adams fired a ball straight into his attacker's heart. She fell over backward with Adams right on top of her, jabbing his knife repeatedly into her chest.

Ben, in the meantime, sorely wounded, bounded back to camp, yowling and leaving a trail of blood. He was followed by his foster brother, Rambler, and his master, who tried in vain to call him to a halt. The young bear was hurt and scared to death by this first battle. The Yankee now realized that he too was badly hurt. Blood was running and dripping all over his greasy buckskins. The she-bear had bitten him deeply in the neck, right through his hunting jacket and a thick flannel shirt. Worse, she had ripped his scalp dreadfully.

Grizzly was barely able to stagger back to camp but, once

there, he attended to Ben, lying under a wagon licking his wounds, before taking care of himself. So sorry did Adams feel for his pet, who had surely saved his life, that he tended the animal like a nurse for a full week. At the end of that length of time, the bear was sufficiently mended to hit the trail again, so Adams struck out for Corral Hollow. When anyone ever asked him why he seemed partial to that particular bear, Adams would tell him of Ben's rushing to his rescue in the Sierra. He would say, "That was one of the narrowest escapes I ever had in all my hunting and, as my preservation was due to Ben, the circumstance explains to some extent the partiality I have felt towards that noble animal. He has borne the scars of the combat upon his front ever since, and I take pride in pointing them out to persons who, I think, can appreciate my feelings towards him."

Back at Adams Springs in the Hollow, Adams recuperated by setting snares for mountain lions. The evening after his arrival, a wild-looking fellow came up as he sat at the campfire and asked permission to camp with him. He looked like a scoundrel to Adams, a pretty fair country judge of character. But the Wild Yankee never turned any man away from his cookfire, good or bad. He rustled up some grub for his mysterious visitor and let him sleep by the fire. Next morning, Adams gave him breakfast and chatted with him, telling him that he was trapping lions in the Hollow. The rough-looking customer, who said that he was one of Livermore's hands (which Adams chose not to believe), left without a word of thanks for Adams's hospitality and only grunted when Adams suggested that he take a look at the lion trap which lay on his route to Livermore's Pass.

An hour or two after breakfast, Grizzly rode his mule out to inspect the trap but, first, he helped a neighbor load some hay. When he eventually reached the trap, after several hours of delay, it was just in time to see a catamount running away. By the time Adams got the butt of his rifle snug against his shoulder, the cat was loping along 200 yards away. He took hurried aim and fired, but at that distance, even Adams could not hit the mark. The puma escaped. Going up to the trap, Adams was astonished to see another mountain lion, lying dead just outside the trap's door. And the cat was minus its tail! Scouting around the pen, Adams was soon able to deduce what had happened. His suspicious-looking visitor had shot the trapped lion in the pen, then dragged its body out and cut off its long tail as a trophy. The New Englander swore like a horse marine and damned his breakfast guest to hell. Spurring his mule into a run, Adams headed for Livermore's Pass, some twelve to fourteen miles away. But, although he rode all day, he did not overtake the stranger and he figured that the rogue had hidden and let him ride right past him, going and coming. How mad Adams was at the stranger! He recalled later, still fuming, "Could I have caught the miscreant at that moment, I would have slaughtered him on the spot."

The Yankee hunter returned to the trap, packed the lion on his mule, and made his way to camp. He did not cater too much to catamount meat but he put great faith in the efficacy of panther oil as liniment for the treatment of bruises and sprains. So he began to butcher the big cat and to prepare it for frying, to render out the oil. While he was cutting up the carcass, a man named Scarf, who was running a sheep ranch a half-dozen miles down the Hollow, happened by.

The shepherd smacked his lips when he saw Adams's panther. "Hello! You have got a fine-looking lion there. You've been very lucky today."

"Yes," agreed Adams, "and the absence of the tail renders it impossible to stuff the hide for exhibition."

The sheepman continued, "Do you know that a California lion is good to eat?"

Adams replied that he believed lion meat was certainly not

the best meat in the world but, on the other hand, neither was it the worst.

"From the look of it, it ought to be good," observed the sheepman. "Now, I'll show you. You get some wood and water while I dress and cook him. I think I can make out of him what you'll admit is an excellent dinner."

Adams and Scarf roasted some of the tenderloin and liver and joined in a jolly supper of lion's meat. After the sheepherder left him, Adams set out to check one of his traps, a mile away. But he never reached it. Long before he was even close, he broke out in a sweat and felt weak and sick. He next became violently ill, dizzy, and nearly blind. The Old Hunter was barely able to stagger into camp. Unluckily, he was alone in camp for a day or so. Neither Combe nor Wright was there to help him. Adams feared that death was finally approaching but he was determined to go down swinging. He tore into his stores till he found his supply of wild tobacco. With this, he made himself a filthy drink which he gulped down. This concoction caused him to vomit violently and repeatedly. After the retching subsided, he rolled up in his blankets to try to sleep. But his throbbing head felt swollen to bursting with pain and the whole night he passed awake but in a kind of delirium of agony. Adams thought that morning would never come. But come it did, and when it did, the Yankee Hunter found that he could not even get to his feet.

He drifted into a doze, finally, and the sun was well up when he was awakened by the sound of a voice. It asked, "Are you sick, too?" Blinking his eyes open, Adams saw that it was one of Scarf's men who spoke to him. He managed to reply that he felt that death had a sure grip on him.

"You are poisoned," said the sheepman.

"Poisoned? That cannot be," expostulated Adams, shaking his pained head. "There's no poison about camp."

But the hired man insisted. "It was the wretch who killed

the panther. He passed our ranch day before yesterday and had a bottle of poison which he showed me. Scarf is poisoned, too, and is suffering in the same manner as yourself."

Comparing notes, Adams and the shepherd figured that the scoundrel had dosed the catamount with strychnine, intended as coyote poison, before killing it with a rifle shot (out of impatience) and cutting off its tail as a trophy. Or, perhaps he had shot the lion and then doctored the wound with some strychnine, to poison the carcass for predatory coyotes.

A few days later, one of the Livermore family told Adams that the fellow had visited the ranch and gone through the Pass, exhibiting the mountain lion's tail and boasting of the desperate struggle in the mountains by which he had won it as a trophy.

The poisoning taught Grizzly a lesson he never forgot—not to eat meat not killed by himself or a friend. And especially to beware meat in a country where phosphorus, arsenic and strychnine were in such common use against everything from squirrels to grizzlies.

His violent vomiting, induced by the vile potion of Indian tobacco, had saved Adams's life. Scarf was spared from an agonizing death, too, but never fully recovered and was still sickly almost six years later. In 1860, Adams said of the poisoner, "I am not very vindictive but it makes my fingers tingle yet whenever I think of the treacherous wretch. I watched for him long and well, but he never, by any chance, came around." Had he come around, there is little doubt that Grizzly Adams would have reduced the population of California by one.

CHAPTER XII

COAST RANGE ADVENTURES

As the flow of Argonauts passed Adams's Spring, the Old Hunter began to think seriously of trying his hand at gold prospecting again in the Kern River placers. Although outwardly he laughed at the new El Dorado as but another of "those periodical visitations of a mild species of insanity," the old gold fever still lurked in his blood. He began preparations although, by the time he was ready, a reverse flow of disappointed miners had set in and traffic toward San Francisco was almost as heavy as that headed for the San Joaquin Valley and the Kern River.

Adams rationalized his gold-hunting trip by combining it with a hunting and exploring expedition through the San Joaquin Valley. He also thought it would be a good idea to try selling meat to the miners. Moreover, in the lonely area en route to the Kern he would have a good chance of capturing some live specimens for his growing menagerie. But mostly, he told himself, he just wanted to see some new country. The Yankee fitted himself out with two horses, besides his span of mules, and loaded the wagon full of such stores as sugar, tea, coffee, tobacco, flour and a keg of whiskey. (The last essential would prove, this trip, to be a curse. For, while he planned to take Combe with him, that lad decided not to go and Adams had to take a stranger, named either

Drury or Carroll, depending on which memoir you read. And the new man proved to be a drunk.) Adams also took packsaddles for Ben Franklin and Lady Washington and did not forget a full mining kit—crowbars, picks, shovels, pans, buckets and miscellaneous tools, plus boards with which to fashion a rocker. Lady Washington traveled along chained to the rear axletree of the wagon, as usual, but Ben and, of course, Rambler were allowed by Grizzly to range freely along the route of march.

Early one sunny morning, Adams and his entourage dropped down Corral Hollow to the flats, then followed the eastern edge of the Coast Range mountains till evening. He camped on the banks of a small stream called the Arroyo Mocho (Cutoff Creek) which, like the Humboldt or the Carson, poured its sparse waters into a flat where they disappeared. Perhaps Adams camped on this creek-without-an-outlet near the spot where the body of Juan Carrasco was found in 1838. The Californian died there, of hunger, in that hot and almost waterless plain. Grizzly found water there, luckily, and took advantage of it to soak his wagon's wheels which were so dry and brittle that not only were the rims falling off but the wheels themselves were in danger of shaking to pieces as he traveled over the roadless ground.

While unhitching the mules and watering and picketing the animals, Adams gave orders to Drury (Carroll) to make supper. It was about an hour later that he checked on his companion's progress. To his intense disgust, he found that the man had addressed himself to the whiskey keg altogether too often and was, in fact, as drunk as a lord. Grizzly had no objection to temperate guzzling but total insobriety on the part of his only companion could wreck his whole expedition. He decided that the most drastic kind of measure was in order. Taking the keg away from Drury/Carroll, he knocked its head in with his ax and let the liquor sink into

157

the sandy soil. He then fixed his supper and ate it before turning in, without a word to his bleary partner.

At midnight, Adams was awakened by his companion calling to him for water. The Yankee refused to crawl out of a warm bed in order to humor a drunk. He told him that, if he wanted water, he could damned well go down to the Arroyo Mocho, himself, and get it. In fact, he could throw himself into the creek and stay there till the liquor was soaked out of his carcass, for all Adams cared. But an hour of grumbling and imploring by his partner softened up Adams's hard New England heart and he got up, fetched him his blankets and gave him water to drink. He then fell asleep after Drury/Carroll finally dozed off.

In the morning, Adams was up bright and early. He fed the animals, then himself, and, ready to move out, called the hung-over Drury. The latter would not—or, perhaps, *could* not—arise. But he could lie there and complain of being deathly sick. This plaint pestered Adams so much that he turned on the hapless lad and tongue-lashed him. He told Drury that he had acted like a hog and that if he was too sick to get on his feet, Adams would jolly well leave him right where he was. This frightening thought finally penetrated Drury's fuzzed mind and he staggered to his feet and stumbled off after the hunter. Adams told him that if he ever took a drink again, he would throw him out of camp. Drury was soon lagging behind Ben and Rambler, could barely sit his horse, and was pitifully pale so Adams took him off his mount and let him ride in the wagon. He stopped early that day and put the sufferer to bed. Leaving him to sleep, Adams took Lady Washington, Ben and Rambler on a hunt which netted three antelope. After taking supper and a cup of strong coffee, Drury felt better and was able to move out early the next morning with Adams and the outfit.

About midday, the greyhound, Rambler, flushed an antelope on the grassy plain between the San Joaquin River on the left and the mountains on the right. It was the beginning of the strangest race that Grizzly had ever seen. The fleet antelope ran toward the faint line of cottonwoods marking the river, far ahead. Rambler kept right on his heels but poor Ben, although he imitated his foster brother as best he could, was simply not built like a greyhound or an antelope. The grizzly soon fell back but he kept loping along, all alone, for another mile before his wind failed him entirely. Adams always remembered how his pet bear looked after he gave up the chase: "He came back with a look on his countenance which showed that he did not wish to be considered as having been in the race."

Using his spyglass, Adams studied the contest between Rambler and the fleeing antelope. The hound kept up with the pronghorn for eight miles but when the antelope reached the screen of bushes and willows and cottonwoods, the dog did not know what to do. Rambler stopped and turned to see if Adams was following. When the dog discovered that his master was not behind him, and that Ben was far, far away, he let the antelope escape. Rambler rejoined Adams in about an hour, apparently very tired. He ran to Ben and jumped and whined about the bear. "It really appeared to me," wrote Adams, later, "that he was trying to tell the bear what a fine race he had had, and was reproaching him for his want of bottom to run." Many times, thereafter, the tame grizzly would take off on a run with Rambler but, of course, was never able to keep up with the racing greyhound for even a half mile.

When Adams camped that night, it was on a ravine—perhaps Orestimba Creek—near the foot of the mountains and close to a large herd of cattle grazing on the vast, unfenced plain. Some *vaqueros,* perhaps from the Crow Ranch (he did not recall, in his memoirs) rode over to talk. After chinning with Grizzly for a time they mounted up and rode over to the ranch, leaving the cattle untended. At sundown, Adams's attention was seized by a commotion among the cattle. He walked over for a look and found that a grizzly was rolling in the grass while the steers gathered around him like a human audience. Adams ran back to camp, grabbed up his rifle, and returned to the scene. He made his way carefully so as not to alarm the bear or spook the cattle. He had heard of grizzlies tricking, or decoying, cattle by one method or another but he had never seen one in action till now. The huntsman settled down in the grass to watch the bear and the near-hypnotized cattle. The grizzly continued its antics, tumbling and frolicking in the long grass, turning half somersaults and even chasing its tail. The foolish cattle bawled but crowded ever closer to the hairy acrobat. A few bulls ran up toward the bear with horns cocked in a threatening manner but always veered off before colliding with bruin. But finally a young heifer imitated her elders and made a run as if to butt or horn the grizzly. In a split second, the bear rose up on its hind legs and caught the cow around the neck with its powerful jaws. In a smooth motion, testimony of long practice, it then shifted its powerful jaws to a grip on the heifer's nose. Jerking its massive head, the bear threw the young cow to the ground, shifted its hold again and bit her savagely in the neck. In only moments, the heifer was dead. She had hardly stopped kicking before the grizzly was busy with supper. The half-wild California cattle drew back, finally realizing that they had been hoodwinked by the show-off bear. But still they stayed in a circle around the feeding bear until the grizzly rushed into their midst. Then, and only then, the strange spell was broken and the cattle stampeded. Adams was not sure if it was mesmerism or a stupid kind of courage which kept the cattle on the scene.

With the cattle scattering to the four winds and the grizzly dashing back and forth to speed them on their way, Adams had no chance to get a good bead on the bear. However, the hunter was so entertained by the strange spectacle that he

High up in the piney Sierra Nevada of California, near the headwaters of the Stanislaus, Tuolumne and Merced rivers, Grizzly Adams set up a series of camps from which he trapped mountain lions and grizzly bears in hunting feats never equaled either before or since his time.

Nevada's State Route 3 follows Grizzly Adams's old trail, in part, near Wellington as it parallels the Walker River on its rushing way to Walker Lake.

When Adams abandoned the Sierra Nevada as his headquarters for hunting and trapping wild animals, to exhibit in American cities, he made a beeline for the peak of the Coast Range looming high above San Francisco Bay, Mount Diablo.

In the caves and crevices of the Coast Range of California, Adams found the hideouts of bears, pumas and even jaguars, in his last great hunting expedition. The hot and brushy range proved to be a hunter's paradise for the Wild Yankee.

Courtesy California State Division of Beaches and Parks

In Corral Hollow and the open, rolling country surrounding it, as different from the steep timbered haunts he had known in the Sierra as night from day, Grizzly found game of all kinds, including the big cats and deadly grizzlies he preferred to trap.

Courtesy California State Division of Beaches and Parks

Burning up with fever on his last great hunt, in the fall of 1855, Grizzly Adams sent his hunting companion to California's old "Earthquake Post," Fort Tejon (above) for help. Instead, the man was trapped by the wiles of the squaws and Mexican girls who hung about the Army post and he left the wild New Englander to fend for himself in the Coast Range.

Grizzly posed for P. T. Barnum in New York with one of his tamed California grizzlies—not Ben Franklin, who had died in San Francisco, but perhaps Lady Washington. The sketch appeared on the cover of the New York biography which made his name a household word in New York as well as on the Pacific Coast.

Courtesy Henry E. Huntington Library

Of great interest to New Yorkers at Grizzly Adams's and Phineas Barnum's American Museum was the California sea lion which Grizzly apparently trapped on or near Seal Rocks, off the famed Cliff House in San Francisco.

Courtesy Henry E. Huntington Library

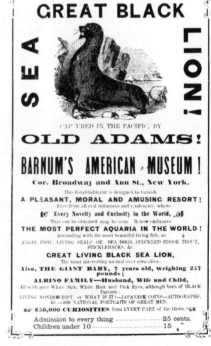

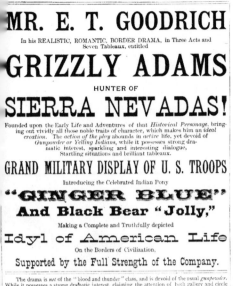

MR. E. T. GOODRICH

In his REALISTIC, ROMANTIC, BORDER DRAMA, in Three Acts and
Seven Tableaux, entitled

GRIZZLY ADAMS

HUNTER OF

SIERRA NEVADAS!

Founded upon the Early Life and Adventures of that *Historical Personage*, bringing out vividly all those noble traits of character, which makes him an *ideal
creation*. The *action of the play* abounds in *active* life, yet devoid of
Gunpowder or Yelling Indians, while it possesses strong dramatic interest, sparkling and interesting dialogue,
Startling situations and brilliant tableaux.

GRAND MILITARY DISPLAY OF U. S. TROOPS

Introducing the Celebrated Indian Pony

"GINGER BLUE"

And Black Bear "Jolly,"

Making a Complete and Truthfully depicted

Idyl of American Life

On the Borders of Civilization.

Supported by the Full Strength of the Company.

The drama is *not* of the "blood and thunder" class, and is devoid of the usual *gunpowder*.
While it possesses a strong dramatic interest, claiming the attention of both gallery and circle
from the first to the close, giving equal satisfaction to both male and female auditors, it is re-
plete with sparkling and interesting dialogue, startling situations and brilliant tableaux. Wherever it has been produced it has been pronounced the *very best* of border dramas.

The above sterling attraction has new and elegant printing, a company carefully selected
to fill the required parts, and an outfit the general excellence of which warrants the assertion
that "GRIZZLY ADAMS" is the Popular Border Drama of the Season.

A faithful ideal of primitive America, when well presented, has always met with the favor
of the people. To this end "GRIZZLY ADAMS," as presented by Mr. Goodrich
and his company, has no opposition; and no expense will be spared to make it an attractive
and picturesque novelty.

*Grizzly Adams, Hunter of Sierra
Nevadas* enjoyed some of its run in
the 1880's by the courtesy of and
subsidy by a patent medicine firm
in New York whose pride and joy
was a nauseous nostrum called
Merchant's Gargling Oil Liniment.

Courtesy California State Library

Courtesy California Historical Society, San Francisco

When Sterrett and Butler published a handbill as a souvenir of the grand
parade in San Francisco to honor the successful laying of the Atlantic Telegraph Cable in September 1858, they could do no less than pose the city's
favorite, Grizzly Adams, with some of his burly pets, in front of their
headquarters.

Dime novel hacks seized upon Grizzly Adams as a hero for their blood-and-thunder epics. This is one cover depiction of Adams in action, racing pell-mell down a Sierra slope in pursuit of a grizzly which he has apparently lassoed, pistols drawn and held in such a fashion that Adams is likely to lose a big toe. (The incident is fictitious, of course.)

did not want to shoot, anyway. But when the grizzly, finally sated, turned away from its meal as if to make off, Adams bellied his way up closer and drew a bead on him. He fired but the distance and failing light sent his ball wild. The report brought the beast to its hind legs, to growl menacingly, but it then wandered off toward the mountains. Adams made no further attempt to detain it.

In the morning, Grizzly sent Drury to report the incident to the *rancheros*. When his companion returned, it was with two of the ranch owners and the *vaqueros* who had paid the call the day before. The two cattlemen told Adams that grizzlies were giving them a lot of trouble and they offered him $100 a month and all the beef he could eat if he would turn predator-hunter for a few months. Adams was confident that he could clean the grizzlies out of the area in jig time but he laughed at the ranch owners' offer, saying, "A gold hunter on his way to Kern River cannot be purchased on terms like these." The other men then laughed, for they had little faith in the Kern River El Dorado. The meeting ended in good-natured banter and the men let Adams take a portion of the dead heifer as he went on his way.

Grizzly wended his way south to a point on the plain near the exit of historic Pacheco Pass, possibly on the property of the old San Luís de Gonzaga Rancho. He camped there, then turned west next morning to investigate the pass through the Coast Range which linked the Salinas and San Joaquin valleys. Through it rushed a blast of cool, turbulent sea air sucked inland by the dry heat of the San Joaquin Valley. He drove the wagon up to a ranch where he found almost a hundred men gathered, both cattlemen and miners. When the crowd saw the bears with Adams, they crowded around the wagon, plying the Yankee with questions. After explaining who he was, where he was from, and whither bound, Grizzly was told that he was off course for the Kern River country. He replied that he knew it, but said that he wanted to investigate some of the mountain cañons. As he talked, he noticed how the men kept eying him and his gear. He figured that they were taking him for a bear hunter dabbling in rustling, because of the suspiciously fresh beef lying on the bed of the wagon. They said nothing hostile but the looks in their eyes spoke volumes.

Finally Adams blurted, "Gentlemen, you look at my beef as if you were hungry. If you desire, you can share it with me, and you will find that it is neither stolen nor poisoned." He then explained about the raiding grizzly.

The story satisfied the men completely, for they were used to the predation of such bears, themselves. They invited Adams to join them at breakfast in the ranch house. Adams declined, with thanks, explaining that he never breakfasted so late in the day. But he did go inside with them and while they ate he peppered them with questions about the way ahead, the cañons, and the valley of which he had heard so much. This was Joaquin's Valley, or Priest's Valley, supposedly rich with game. The men told him that the valley was named after the Mexican-Californian bandit, Joaquín Murieta, and that its other name came from the fact that some of the first Anglos into it had come upon a *padre* and a hundred Mission Indians rounding up wild horses. According to the cattlemen, Priest's Valley lay about three days' journey south via a particularly rugged road. In fact, they doubted that there was enough of a trail for a wagon to get through. Certainly none, to their knowledge, had tried it before Adams's rig.

Grizzly Adams was already aware of the remoteness and desolation of Priest's Valley. Few men—and fewer Anglo-Californians—stayed there long, except horse rustlers like Peg Leg Smith. He did not need the information of the ranchers to know that it had been the hangout of Joaquín Murieta and his band of cutthroats until they were virtually wiped out in a battle with Captain Harry Love's California

Rangers at Arroyo de Cantúa, to the east, in 1853. But they tried to dissuade him from going to Priest's Valley mostly because no one knew if all of the bandits had left it. Chances were good that some of Murieta's stragglers were still holed up in the hidden valley. To this warning, Adams replied, "It is not certain that any of them are there and, anyway, our danger is nearly as great in any part of this country as another, so far as thieves go." He chose to ignore the well-meant warning.

Taking his leave of the friendly cowmen, Adams started out again, bypassing (unwittingly) Panoche Pass and the Pinnacles, far to the west, and seeing little of interest that day but three or four ranches and a few wild mustangs. However, the next day's journey brought him to a high hill or *picacho* of which the ranchers had spoken as the jumping-off place for Priest's Valley. This may have been 4,858-foot San Carlos Peak or one of the neighboring summits of the New Idria quicksilver country. On this high point of the cordillera named, again, for bloody Murieta—Joaquin Ridge—Adams scanned the country to the west and south with his glass.

A thousand feet below him lay a large and grassy plain, Joaquin's or Priest's Valley. It was rather level and through it meandered a stream outlined by a growth of cottonwoods. The valley was literally dotted with grazing antelope and wild horses. The slope which slanted down from his perch toward the distant creek was nearly a cliff, it was so steep. Bounded at the top with a fringe of scrub brush and littered at the bottom with boulders, it would not be an easy task to get down that slope . . . even without a heavily loaded wagon and two pet grizzly bears! But there was nothing to be done but to try it.

Adams led his horses down first, planning to do the same for Lady Washington. But the ascent was so tiring that he decided to bring everything and everyone down in one fell swoop. The puffing Adams locked two of the wagon's wheels while, under his orders, Drury took hitches around trees at the top of the near-precipice with a line made of their strongest lariats lashed together and tied to one of the axletrees. With the bears aboard and the mules in harness, Adams and Drury began to slacken the line, lowering the wagon down the slope as if they were warping a boat from its dock. Paying out line carefully, the two men worked the wagon, mules and bears (and themselves) halfway down the slope when, gradually, the wagon began to swing broadside to the mountain. A quick command from Adams sent Drury atop one of the inside wheels where his weight kept the vehicle upright. But after skidding downhill a few hundred feet farther, *crash!* the wagon and whole shebang overturned, spewing out men, gear and bears.

When things quieted down and the dust had settled, Adams examined the damage. First he calmed Lady Washington who was thrown so violently from her seat that, when she landed, she plowed a furrow in the soft earth with her muzzle. The Lady was so frightened that her hair stood on end and she was snuffing and snorting agitatedly till her master cooled her off by stroking her and patting her on the head. Soon she was relaxed and licking Adams's hand. This signified, in Adams's mind at least, that she forgave him for the accident.

With Lady Washington settled down, Adams turned next to the shipwrecked wagon. He replaced a tire iron which had come off and managed to repair the broken-off wagon tongue by chopping two pieces of oak and lashing them to the stub of the tongue with lariats and thongs of green hide. While he was busy with this work, he had Drury collecting the scattered baggage and packing it on the mules to the valley below. Finally, Adams mended the torn harness with rawhide and buckskin so that, by nightfall, he and Drury had the wagon safely down on the valley floor, all reloaded.

During their descent, capsizing and recovery, the men and

animals had not had a drop of water to drink and they were suffering badly from thirst in the hot sun. Since they were still some distance from the line of timber marking the stream, Adams allowed no one any rest, for he saw that they could not reach it before evening. It was clear, starry night before they reached the cottonwoods, tortured by thirst, only to find the stream bed completely dry. The Pacheco Pass folk had warned him that he would find only pools of water in the watercourse at this season but they had not dreamed that he would find a completely dry bed. Adams walked along the sandy bed for some distance. From its appearance, he guessed that it was typical of the Southern California waterways which rose and sank every few miles. He was sure that the underground stream would come to the surface again, farther along.

Remounting, Grizzly ordered Drury to walk along the creek bed, searching for a pool of water, while he drove the team along the bank. The thirsty Drury almost mutinied here. He demanded to know why he had to walk and not ride. Patiently, the Yankee explained to him that there were two very good reasons. First, the banks of the arroyo were steep and it would be difficult to get a horse down into the stream bed or back out of it again. And, second, Drury could travel on foot over the soft and loose sand better than on horseback. Drury muttered his opposition but did as Grizzly bade him, literally throwing himself down the steep creek bank.

Adams drove onward for nearly an hour without seeing Drury again or hearing a word out of him. Finally, he began to worry about his companion deserting him. He recalled, "A thousand suspicions, indeed, passed through my mind, as is usual when we have no confidence in persons whom we are compelled to trust."

At last, Drury reappeared, pushing his way through a clump of bushes on the edge of the creek bank. He reported water under some rocks in a deep part of the ravine. The bank there was too steep, on Adams's side of the stream, to descend but the other bank, with a gentler slope, could be reached only after a long and roundabout detour. Grizzly realized that his tired animals were not up to any more travel. He ordered a stop and he and Drury began to laboriously haul water up the steep bank to the animals. But Ben and Rambler were not as tuckered out as they seemed. As soon as they saw—or smelled—the water, they crashed down the steep cut to wallow up to their middles in the pool while they quenched their thirst. Adams reckoned that it had been a pretty fatiguing twenty-four hours and he told Drury that they would camp right where they were for a full day of rest. He and his partner then spread their blankets on the ground in the shade of the cottonwoods, for the sun was already climbing, and dropped off into an enjoyable sleep.

When Adams awoke, it was midafternoon. He decided not to stay any longer where they were but to push ahead to the valley itself, which they had not quite reached. He and Drury had the animals hitched when their attention was caught by the strange actions of the dog and Ben. Taking up his rifle, Adams retraced his steps to the pool. Sure enough, there was a band of antelope drinking there. He fired and dropped one but the others, with the speed of wind, were up and out of the creek in a flash and streaking across the plain toward the distant San Joaquin River. Adams sicked the dog and bear on them and both animals tore off as if shot from guns. But, shortly, Ben slowed down his loping and turned to see if Adams was following. Finding that he was not in on the pursuit, the bear returned and sat down on his haunches where Adams was skinning out the antelope. Too well-trained to snatch anything, Ben still grumbled for food when he was hungry. Wrote Adams, later, "I shall never forget how he sat there, wistfully eyeing my carving, looking into my face, and remonstrating about my strictness with him. . . . I resolved to try him a little and placed food in such a way as to tempt him, but the faithful fellow continued true to his training, and the meat remained inviolate." Finally, Adams threw him the entrails and the grizzly ate until Adams thought he would burst.

Loading the antelope meat on the wagon, Adams gave the command and the little party moved out, traveling fast until sundown when they were well within the mouth of Priest's Valley itself. It was approached via a rugged side cañon so plugged with rocks that the wagon was barely able to enter. Here Adams ordered camp set up. Next morning, they proceeded up the valley proper. To do so, they had to cross the creek in it at least a dozen times and once they had to unload the wagon, to boot. But it was well worth the effort, for, as Adams recalled, "We found one of the most beautiful valleys in all California. It was about six miles long by one wide, covered with grass and grove-like clumps of trees, and surrounded by mountains which, in some places, were so precipitous that it was impossible for a man to climb them. In the center of the valley was a ridge of slightly elevated land, dividing into two branches the stream which sprang from fountains at its head. A stock raiser could not desire a finer location and had I not been a hunter of wild animals, I should certainly have wished to settle down here, and devote my attention to the rearing of domestic ones."

After pitching camp and eating dinner under some fine oaks, Adams took his rifle and, followed by Ben and Rambler as usual, set out for the nearest flank of the mountains which locked in the valley. Soon Rambler showed uneasiness and Ben began sniffing the air. This meant bear! Shortly, Adams discovered a female grizzly and two cubs feeding in the bushes. He made his animals lie still, then he crept forward and with a single shot killed the dam. Ben and Rambler rushed forward, unable to hold themselves, after Adams shot one of the cubs. They seized the surviving cub, Rambler by one leg and Ben by the neck, and shook the animal terribly. Adams called them off and tried to save the cub for his menagerie but it died of its injuries.

The following day, Adams and Drury killed a couple of antelope and then climbed a high peak at the head of Priest's Valley. It was an odd-looking peak, with slab-sided rocks clinging to its sides. From its top, he hoped to spy some of the wild cattle he had heard of. When he and Drury reached the summit, they found a wonderful viewpoint. They could not see the Pacific Ocean but waves of mountain ridges stretched toward the sundown horizon. On the east, a range of hills blocked a view of the San Joaquin Valley but beyond that plain they could see the line, like a second horizon in that quarter, which was the Sierra Nevada.

On their descent, the two hunters encountered some of the wild cattle which they sought. Adams thought that they were the most savage-looking of all animals he had ever seen. He had always thought that the cattle he had seen in Mexico were longhorns but they could not compare with these California critters. "The cattle themselves were extraordinarily large, and having these immense horns, with shaggy hair about the shoulders and head, they presented an appearance almost terrific." Somewhat to his surprise, however, the dangerous-looking beasts immediately fled upon seeing the two men. Since it was nearing nightfall, Adams did not pursue them but, instead, led Drury on the way back to their snug camp in Priest's Valley.

CHAPTER XIII

VALLEY OF THE TULES

$\mathbf{S}$LIPPING and sliding, the two hunters made their way down from the brush-covered hogback. As their camp came into view on the valley floor below them, Adams waved Drury to a halt. At first, the Yankee thought that his eyes were deceiving him. He brought up his spyglass. No, it was true; grouped around their campfire were a half-dozen rough-looking men and their horses!

Grizzly's mind immediately raced back to the dire warnings the Pacheco Pass folk had given him. These must be members of Joaquín Murieta's old gang of bloodthirsty brigands! Once the surprise wore off, Adams was, as usual, unafraid of man or beast, so he led Drury right into camp, rifles ready for action. To his relief—and particularly to Drury's—he found that the strangers were both peaceable and friendly. They welcomed him and his companion to the fire that twinkled in the dusk. After shaking hands all around, Adams learned that the two Americans were from San Francisco and on their way to the nearby New Idria quicksilver mines. The five swarthy men were Spanish-Californians and mustangers. They had their corrals for wild horses down in the San Joaquin, near Tulare Lake, and had heard about Grizzly from the *vaqueros* of Pacheco Pass. They had deliberately sought his camp in order to get some meat. The weather-worn horse hunters were amused when Adams told them that he had taken them for members of Murieta's old band of outlaws. They laughed and assured him that none of Joaquín's men were in the vicinity any longer.

Next morning, the Hispano-Californians left but the two Americans prevailed on the Yankee hunter to join them on a visit to the quicksilver workings, only ten miles or so distant. As an ex-miner himself, Adams was most agreeable to the suggestion and he spent a day at New Idria, inspecting the mines and picking up specimens of cinnabar for souvenirs. The San Franciscans told him that the ore was good and that, one day, the little-worked mines would be very valuable. Adams recalled that day to reporter Hittell in San Francisco, long after, "I often think that, had I only sat down and taken up the valley, I might now have been a kind of monarch, the possessor of a beautiful little kingdom with uncounted herds and flocks on every side. But such was not my destiny."

He found the mines all but deserted. An old Spanish-Californian, or Mexican, was in sole charge, his *compañeros* having gone to San Luis Obispo for supplies. The Mexican joined Adams and Drury/Carroll and the two city men for a day or two of elk hunting. The old-timer knew a cañon where the wapiti were bound to be found, if there were any elk in the entire area. He told Adams that if the ravine was deserted, he could be sure that all animals in the vicinity would have gone to the *tulares* (reed plains and swamps) near Tulare Lake in the middle of the San Joaquin Valley, to escape the fly season of summer.

The *Californio* led Adams and the others to the ravine and pointed out a dozen or fifteen elk, including about six young. Grizzly was keen on capturing some of the youngsters to exhibit while he killed some of the adult animals for meat. He gave the Mexican the horse and several lassos while he posted Drury on guard at the mouth of the wash. Then Adams himself crept up through the buckbrush until he was quite close to the grazing herd. He wanted to try the "flag trick" on elk, since it had worked so well for him with antelope. Tying his red silk handkerchief on the end of a stick, he raised the bandanna and, at the same time, whistled in a pretty fair imitation of an elk call. The animals stopped their eating and gazed fixedly at Adams's little red flag. Slowly they approached as their curiosity was whetted. The concealed hunter fired through the bushes and brought down the nearest animal. The others appeared bewildered by the noise and smoke and the accident which had befallen their comrade, but still they came on while Adams reloaded and fired again, wounding a second one. A third time he was able to reload without spooking the herd. He fired again and wounded a third animal. This elk gave a bleat as it was hurt and the Mexican took the sound for Adams's agreed-upon signal. He went into action, spurring his horse and charging like a dragoon at the herd. It scattered, of course, but not before the oldster had dropped a loop around the neck of one small animal. Adams ran forward and took the lasso while the Mexican built a loop in another reata and urged his mount down the arroyo after the retreating animals. He was able to rope another young elk and bring him to camp. Grizzly was pleased with his three dead adult wapiti and two live fawns.

The Mexican proved to be a very satisfactory hunting companion for the particular and finicky Adams so, after they had prepared the elk meat for jerking, or drying, next day, Adams took him out again. They clambered up the high hogback, hoping to find some of the wild cattle Adams had seen before. It was not long before they ran into a herd of fifteen or twenty of them. Since Adams knew that the *Californio*, like all of his breed, was an expert with the lasso, he suggested that he rope one. But the Mexican balked, saying that the ground was too rough for cattle as strong and wild as these. So Adams gave up the idea of capturing a wild longhorn alive. Instead, he began to stalk them, snaking up through the grass to a natural blind of some rocks. He fired at the foremost bull and wounded it so badly that it could not keep up with its fleeing fellows. Adams then shot it again and killed it. When he examined the animal carefully, he found that the bull differed so much from regular cattle that he almost felt that the feral longhorns belonged to a new species. Actually, several generations of reversion to a wild state had given the animals thicker hides, much longer horns, and heavier and shaggier coats than their bovine relatives of the lowlands. Too, Adams remarked that their eyes resembled more those of the buffalo than domesticated cattle. Most striking, of course, were the horns; they were enormous. Adams later regretted that he did not pack out the bull's horns for trophies along with the meat which he took. They would have been most interesting curiosities in the East, well worth exhibiting with his wild beasts.

Next morning, Adams broke camp to resume his march southward to the Kern River, after giving the Mexican some farewell presents. Hitching up, he and Drury led their growing menagerie out of Priest's Valley by the route by which they had entered and headed across a waterless, sandy plain toward the distant San Joaquin River. After fully thirty miles of travel in the hot sun across what was to Adams a desert, no matter what the maps might call it, the Yankee found himself still far from reaching the river or any other source of water, apparently. The sand all but swallowed up the wagon's wheels and progress was miserably slow. All, men and animals, were fatigued but the bears suffered more than horses, mules, dog or men from the punishing thirst of the passage. Ben Franklin was in a particularly bad way from heat and thirst and Adams finally felt compelled to make a dry stop, to succor him. He sent Drury ahead to look for water, on horseback, taking a leather water *bota*.

After a brief rest, Adams resumed his march but very,

very slowly, so that the line of cottonwoods seemed to get no nearer. Even the slow pace of the jaded mules was too much for Ben, who gave out completely. Adams wound pieces of cloth, like bandages, around the bear's badly blistered paws but the grizzly refused to go a step farther. So Grizzly sat down to wait for Drury, keeping a watchful and worried eye on his big pet. Finally, the despair of the grizzly's expression demanded that he do something. He gave up reproaching himself for not bringing enough water and wrenched off some boards from the wagon. With these, brush, and a large blanket, he made a rude *ramada* to shade the animals. Then, leaping into the driver's seat, he urged the mules and wagon toward the distant San Joaquin River.

In a matter of only five miles, he met Drury, returning not from the San Joaquin but a closer spring or water hole. Adams tossed him the reins and changed places with him, ordering him to drive on to the water source at a slow pace, to spare the mules. Adams's thoughts were all on Ben; he galloped back to where he had left the grizzly. Ben lay just as he had left him. Adams gave him several quarts of water, which revived him, but he could not get Ben to move, neither by begging nor beating him. Returning to Drury, whom he found asleep at the spring, Adams awoke him and got him to help unload the wagon and hitch the mules to it again. The two men then rode back to rescue Ben Franklin and the other animals but in the gathering darkness lost their way and spent the whole night trying to find the bear. It was almost daylight when Adams finally spied the blanket awning. Again he gave Ben water and again the grizzly could not walk. But he was able to clamber into the wagon with the help of Adams and Drury tugging and hauling on his 400-pound frame.

So serious was the grizzly's condition that Adams decided to camp for two days at the little spring while he doctored him and made moccasins for him and Lady Washington as he had done on the Humboldt Desert of Nevada. Adams used tough buckskin lined on the inside with soft, tanned leather. He poured bear oil into the boots, then bound them tightly to Ben's feet, hoping that this treatment would cure the blisters which afflicted him and would prevent new ones from forming. This time, he took the added precaution of muzzling his grizzly friend so that he could not tear off the moccasins with his teeth.

The moccasins worked well, Ben improved, and on the third day, Adams drove on to the edge of Tulare Lake, the largest of several lakes at the head of the San Joaquin Valley (now virtually drained away) which had led the pioneer explorer of the area, Pedro Fages, to describe the great *llano,* or plain, as "a labyrinth of lakes and tulares." It was a huge lake, shallow, and surrounded by miles of tule and cattail swamps. The Indians called the lake Chintache; the Spanish-Californians, *Laguna de los Tulares,* but since Frémont's day Anglo-Californians had dubbed it Tulare Lake.

Adams and his cavalcade crossed some sloughs with water in them but nothing resembling the large stream which should drain out of Tulare Lake to feed the San Joaquin River. Far off to the east he could see a line of trees which marked the Kings River. The party was welcomed to Tulare Lake by the whistling of elk on all sides, though hidden by the dense growth of tules. But even these hints of fresh meat aplenty failed to interest, much less stop, Adams. He kept on past the end of the lake until he reached the shelter of the timber on the Kings. He soon found that the Kings River, farther up, ran sluggishly through rolling but barren country with little trees. Accidentally, he had picked the best site in which to camp. There he rested his animals and made the bears more comfortable moccasins out of elkskin.

During the several days of rest on the banks of the Kings, Adams and Drury killed several elk and captured one young fawn. They visited an Indian village of about a hundred souls on the border of Tulare Lake near the mouth of the Kings. Grizzly was able to hire two boys to take him and Drury, by canoe, to an island in the lake where he had heard there were many elk and also various birds in tremendous numbers. It was a matter of almost a mile of slogging through water and tules until they reached open water and the canoe. It was a crude craft, constructed of several logs fastened together and calked with mud and tules.

When they reached the small island, Adams found it was wooded and densely populated by birds in incredible variety —geese, swans, ducks, cranes, curlews, snipe, and fowl he could not identify. Eggs by the thousands lay in the grass and tules. While the Indian boys busied themselves gathering eggs in the reeds, Adams and Drury set out after elk. Adams soon killed one and Drury wounded one. But when Drury, after reloading, pursued the animal, the big wapiti turned on him and crashed down upon him, driving him into the mud like a tent stake. With Drury bellowing for help, Adams took careful aim and shot the elk dead. But then Adams's quixotic nature showed itself again and instead of commiserating with his filthy companion for his discomfiture and narrow escape with his life, he broke out in great guffaws of laughter at Drury's plight. Naturally, Drury found Adams's hilarity quite offensive and pouted so sulkily that Grizzly had to do all the hunting thereafter. Drury just sat glumly, caked in mud.

During the creeping and crawling through the reeds, Adams happened upon an elk fawn only a few days old. He pounced on the baby and seized it, muzzling its jaws when it bleated for parental help. He managed to get the fawn into the canoe along with the elk meat, eggs and Indians, then coaxed a dour Drury aboard. When Adams returned to the village, he was surrounded by all the braves who would not hear one word less than the full story of the successful hunt. Adams was in fine fettle and gave them a good spiel, for, as he later recalled, "Altogether, this island hunt was as pleasant and interesting to me as any I had enjoyed during the season."

Continuing their journey the next day, Adams and Drury drove the wagon over a barren area between the tule marshes to starboard and the foothills and the whitish skyline of the High Sierra to port. They surprised a band of spirited mustangs and gave chase but the wild horses easily showed them their hooves. The next day's march brought them to the Four Creeks area, a real oasis of the San Joaquin in the best sense. Like so many other travelers, both before him and after him, Adams was much taken by the Kaweah country—"There was scenery of a very beautiful description and a country rich, well timbered and well stocked with game." It was truly a happy hunting ground but Adams was so well supplied with meat that he saw no advantage in tarrying there, so he pushed on till he reached the area of the Kern River strike, where he camped.

His first day in the Kern River mines, Grizzly spent talking with prospectors and looking at their claims. From a close examination of their returns during the next few days— rather than their optimistic hopes—he concluded that the Kern placers, rather than constituting a bonanza, would become a borrasca, or bust, if they were not a humbug, entirely. He wrote in 1860, "After digging for eight days, Carroll [i.e., Drury] and I found no more gold than I could put in my eye." But Adams was heartened by the prospects of profit for a competent market hunter, which he knew himself to be. So he decided to start, at once, on this venture, leaving mining to his customers. Fording the Kern early one morning, he proceeded with Drury/Carroll, Ben and Rambler for some ten miles into the higher mountains.

Adams was searching for the area's legendary "red bears." They turned out to be grizzlies and he found three of them rooting about in a chaparral thicket. The hunters, pet bear and greyhound all got within sixty or seventy yards of their prey without being seen or heard, but the bears began to sense (probably, smell) danger and all raised themselves up on their great hind legs. They made just the kind of target which Grizzly Adams liked. He fired and bored the foremost bear right through the heart. Before the animal had expired, Adams had grabbed Drury's rifle and was firing again. The third animal escaped, unscathed, so Adams urged Ben and Rambler to finish off the wounded second bear. A brisk combat ensued, largely between Ben and his wild cousin. When Adams rushed forward to join Rambler and Ben, the bloodied grizzly gave up the unequal battle and fled.

Ben and the greyhound were soon in hot pursuit, with Adams to the rear. Down a ravine they all plunged and when Adams caught up, he found his pets had brought bruin to bay with its back to a dark hole choked with chaparral and rocks. After a quick reloading, Adams shot again but hurried his aim too much and missed. The rifle's report sent the bear into flight again, with Ben and Rambler clinging to its heels.

After a half mile more of running, the country became more and more rough so Adams called back the greyhound and his pet grizzly. To his surprise, he found that the first grizzly had vanished. He had only wounded it, too. A bloody track led off into the brush and Ben and Rambler were quickly on the trail. When Adams caught up with them, he found them nosing the carcass of a giant grizzly in the bottom of an arroyo near a pool of water. It was one of the largest bears Adams had ever seen and he marveled at its strength and valor. The grizzly, shot through the heart, had run a full 300 yards before collapsing and dying. For a moment, Adams was glad that he had called off his rash pursuit of the other two bears. Later, he would ascribe this momentary feeling of timidity to the fact that he was out of practice: "It was my first bear fight for several weeks."

The hunter returned to the mines to sell the bear meat, and also some venison, then went hunting again. This time he came upon a cowardly she-grizzly, the first he had ever encountered. When he fired and wounded her, the mother abandoned her cubs. Adams was almost outraged by this show of cowardice, observing that it was "an action which a bear of more northern latitudes would not be guilty of." He blamed Southern California: "It is only in the south, where heat enervates the species, that such despicable natures exist." With the help of Rambler (Ben having gone off in vain pursuit of the wounded dam), Adams captured both cubs for future exhibit in San Francisco and at Barnum's American Menagerie in New York.

A few evenings later, Ben had another chance. When Adams took a mule out by night to pick up a deer which he had shot earlier, the tame grizzly tagged along. They surprised a grizzly feeding on Adams's buck. The hunter's shot wounded the bear seriously and Ben and Rambler rushed to the attack. An even fight between wild and tame grizzly ensued, with Rambler doing little but annoy the wounded animal. Although it was dark, it was not hard for Adams to keep track of the adversaries because Ben's coat was much darker than his opponent's. When Ben hurled his adversary to the ground Adams decided to step in and stop the fight for good. He did so with a pistol shot followed by a knife thrust. The hunter was proud that Ben Franklin had more than held his own with his wild cousin and felt that in a fair fight, even with the wild bear not wounded, Ben would have emerged the victor.

When the meat business grew a little slow, Adams decided to strike camp. He and Drury/Carroll had netted $77 each from their hunting. He decided to strike farther south, for Tejon Pass, the gateway to southernmost California through the rugged Tehachapi Mountains.

CHAPTER XIV

TEJON PASS COUNTRY

THE chief lure of the sunbaked and barren Tehachapi Mountains to Adams was the legend of its fauna, especially the famed red or cinnamon bears which prowled that range's cañons. Here, where the Coast Ranges collided violently at the desert edge of the San Joaquin Valley with the westering High Sierra, Adams expected to find new and high adventure. When he arrived within thirty miles of Tejon Pass, the main route to Los Angeles and all of Southern California, he and Drury/Carroll camped. Within a short time and almost without incident, Adams and Rambler were able to capture two live cubs. (Overeager Ben killed one, trying to help.)

But that same lucky day changed its character, however, and Adams was laid low with an attack of malaria or some similar affliction. Waves of chills alternated with bouts of high fever. After sending his companion to Fort Tejon for quinine, the grizzly hunter dragged his bed into an opening where the sun would play most of the day. He piled all of his clothes and skins atop his bedroll and then crawled in, trying to sleep away his sickness. But sleep was soon replaced by delirium and in this state he rolled and tossed, tortured by horrible nightmares as well as violent headaches. He saw himself in these Gothic dreams dying on the Colorado Desert;

fighting, single-handed, all the judges and Philadelphia lawyers of Sonora; combating a huge and omnipotent grizzly;
and, lastly, as a condemned man awaiting his doom in a
torture chamber.

The Wild Yankee was awakened from his stupor by a
violent, but kindly, shaking. Through a haze of fever which
obscured sight and sound, he made out someone bending
over him and calling out, "*Americano! Americano!*" Adams
managed to prop himself up on an elbow, to find that his
visitor was an elderly Spanish-Californian. The Mexican explained that he was on his way to the Tulare country from
the Tejon. He asked permission to stay the night at Adams's
camp. Grizzly, grateful for company, of course agreed. By
now, the hunter was again in full command of his senses and
he explained his illness to the *paisano*. The latter averred
that he could cure his new gringo friend and he speedily set
to work to effect this end. He began brewing a decoction of
boiling water, willow bark and red pepper. He ordered
Adams to swallow a draft of this vile stuff. After a tentative
sip, Grizzly protested that it was too hot. The *Californio*
curtly replied that it was just right and he made Adams
worry down the whole cup of it. After thus dosing his patient,
the old man made himself some coffee and turned in. Adams
slept quietly till midnight when two more Spanish-Californians rode up and politely asked if they might spend the
night. This was a request which Adams never refused, and
he told them to dismount and to help themselves to supper.
Soon all the men were asleep.

Once again—but suddenly and violently, this time—Adams
was roused from his slumber. The old Mexican let out a yell
which would have cut through ice. The piercing scream sent
the old hunter to his feet, wobbly as he was. For a moment,
he forgot his sickness and, rifle in one hand and bowie knife
in the other, he prepared to face murderers or worse. The
starlight was feeble and although he could see movement

among his *Californio* visitors Adams could not tell if foul play had been done, or just what. In a loud voice he demanded to know what the commotion was all about. One of the Mexicans answered, "The old man has been bitten by a tarantula."

Like many men of his day—including all of the company at the campsite—Adams had a superstitious awe and fear of the villainous-looking (but relatively harmless) spider. He recalled, later: "The very name of this poisonous spider shocked my whole system and caused the blood to run cold to the extremities of my body. The idea of the miserable death he would have to die almost overpowered me. For a few minutes, I had not the power to move to his relief."

When the moment of shock wore off, Adams grabbed a burning brand from the fire and, using it as a torch, illuminated the circle of men. The old-timer, in truth, looked to be halfway over the jamb of death's door. He was gasping and moaning, pale as a corpse. Adams, along with the others, gave him up as moribund but, mechanically, turned the man's blankets to seek out the hairy and supposedly deadly spider, remarking that he had seen no tarantulas in the area. From the folds of the blankets fell the insect which had stabbed Adams's visitor. It was not the hirsute spider which he expected to see but a different breed of vermin entirely—a scorpion.

Grizzly exclaimed, "It's a scorpion!"

The old man repeated it—"*Un escorpión!*"—and immediately brightened, knowing that the scaly insect's sting was not normally fatal.

His companions meanwhile, with Adams, examined the wound and found it inflamed and swollen but located on an area of his thigh which was apparently remote from any artery or vein.

The other Mexicans suggested that tobacco be applied to the wound but Grizzly said, "I have something better."

Rummaging in his gear, he came up with a supply of the weed which the Indians had prescribed for rattlesnake bite. Just to be doubly sure, he mixed it with a plug of tobacco and applied the mess to the wound as a poultice before binding up the old fellow's fevered thigh. Adams then gave his doctor-turned-patient a dose of tea made of the snakebite preventive. By the next day, after a quiet and long sleep, the old Mexican was almost himself again. He ate a hearty meal of roast bear and pronounced it *muy bueno*. Within another day, he was cured.

Adams's own cure was a slower campaign. He continued doctoring and dosing himself according to the Mexican's pharmacopoeia. Upon feeling the first chill of an oncoming attack of the malaria, ague, or whatever it was, the New Englander would drink a strong infusion of his medicine. This treatment seemed to break the course of the disease and to hasten its demise rather than his own. But, impatient, Adams returned to his customary hydrotherapy. He dragged himself to the creek each time a fever came upon him in order not only to drink heartily but to dunk his head and shoulders repeatedly in the stream. After thus inviting pneumonia, Adams confided to his journal: "This treatment, although contrary, perhaps, to all the rules of therapeutics, worked admirably." In fact, Adams claimed that he never again suffered from chills and fever after that Tehachapi attack.

Blaming his ague on the malarious miasmas of the nearby Tulare marshes, Adams made ready to break camp and ascend the dry mountains as soon as he regained his strength. From travelers, he learned that his emissary to the medicine chests of Fort Tejon, the old "earthquake post," had let him down, as usual. Drury/Carroll, in fact, had deserted him and spent his money on liquor and vice at the hands of a gaggle of squaws and Mexican women at Tejon.

On his last night in camp below the mountains, Adams was surprised when who should walk into the circle of firelight but his strayed companion. A dumfounded Adams heard himself greeted as if absolutely nothing had happened. Drury/Carroll was afoot and, either not noting, or else ignoring, Grizzly's bristling attitude, he immediately launched into a story of having "lost" his mule—which had gone the way of his money, actually. These lies only added insult to injury, so Adams cut him off short and recalled his beastly conduct from the very beginning of the expedition. Ashamed and abashed, the young man stood mute before him. Adams had half a mind to send him away but it was such a wild place that he decided it would be inhuman. So, grudgingly, he permitted the contrite youth to stay.

Next morning, the two men packed up and advanced into the mountains. After several days of wending their way over the twisting route which would one day be descriptively called the Grapevine, they reached a gorge leading out to the southern slopes of the mountains. They camped as near the spring at the head of the wash as the wagon could approach. From there, the lunar landscape of the Mojave Desert's extension of the Great Basin lay stretched before their eyes, like a sandy sea. Far to the west, out of sight, lay the Los Angeles Plain and the Pacific Ocean. At this camp, the two men turned in early for a much-needed rest after the fatigues of the Tehachapi crossing.

It was dark, perhaps midnight, when light-sleeping Adams was roused by a nervous snuffing and snorting among his animals. Knowing nothing more than that there was danger at hand, he groped for his rifle and, cocking the hammer, brought it to a position of readiness. There were stars overhead but they released too little light that night for Adams to see anything distinctly. He would have to depend on his hearing. In a few minutes his ears picked up the sound of lapping at the spring some fifty yards above camp. Grizzly stared in that direction till his eyes adjusted to the gloom and he made out two glaring eyes, like balls of fire. Adams braced himself for an attack but the beast, whatever it was, uttered only a low growl and disappeared. It was plain that the beast not only had no fear of man but did not even deign to attack the likes of Adams. The hunter got only a fleeting glance at the prowling creature. Of only one thing was he sure: it was a giant cat of some kind.

The glimpse of the nocturnal prowler tantalized Adams. What was this beast, some sort of mountain lion? Dictating his memoirs to journalist-amanuensis Hittell, Adams recalled, much later, "During the remainder of the night I could think of nothing else. My imagination presented me with the picture of an animal whose capture could exceed in interest all the adventures of my previous days."

Hardly was it light before the hunter was on the beast's trail, leaving his craven companion to tend the camp. The track wandered over four or five miles of crannied, craggy country, as rough as any Adams had ever seen. It ended in a gorge. The only way into this cul-de-sac was for Grizzly to pull himself painfully along a cliffside. His pet grizzly and the greyhound bungled along behind him at the base of the cliff, as best they could, by a roundabout route. Here and there amid the rocks and rubble were patches of soft earth where Adams's keen eyes picked up enough cat tracks to keep him on the trail. Finally, crossing the head of the gorge, Adams came up against a ledge of rocks and saw the animal's den. In its mouth and below it was a veritable garbage heap of bones and skulls of animals including the unmistakable remains of mountain sheep. To Adams, it looked like the yard of a slaughterhouse. Gingerly advancing toward the cave's mouth, half-seeking and half-fearing a meeting with the proprietor of the abattoir, Adams was at last turned back by the steepness of the cliff. He simply could not reach the mouth of the den. The only thing to do was to build a trap for the giant feline. But even this was no easy matter, for no trees grew in the rock and brush-choked box cañon.

Climbing out of the gorge with great difficulty, Adams reconnoitered along a ridge until he found a timbered valley about four miles from him and some eight or ten miles from the lair. The hour was much too late to accomplish anything so he turned back to camp.

On his way, Adams stumbled on a flock of forty to fifty mountain sheep. Although they were very wary they did not hear him or the (for once) silent approach of his strange companions. Shushing the grizzly and greyhound, Grizzly Adams crept up on them. All the while that they were feeding off bunches of grass they kept a careful watch. Closing in on the bighorns, Adams raised up a bit and fired. To his surprise, two of the bighorns dropped with the one shot. Then he remembered that he had placed an extra-heavy charge in his Kentucky rifle, expecting to have to use it on the giant cat. Examining the two downed sheep, he found that the heavy slug of lead had pierced the heart of the foremost animal and then had passed right on through its body to imbed itself in the neck of the second bighorn.

Dressing out the meat, Grizzly led his four-footed companions on toward camp. But now their heels were dogged by a pack of coyotes, thirsting for the bloody meat Adams was packing. At first, Grizzly tried to ignore the impudence of these wild dogs but finally their saucy yelping got on his nerves. He sicked Ben and Rambler on them and the pack of pursuers seemed to explode apart. The leader was seized by both Ben and Rambler and torn to pieces. The rest of the cowardly band fled to all points of the compass and Adams made his way to camp undisturbed.

Next day, Adams removed his camp to the wooded cañon, where he was lucky enough to find good water and forage. This served as his forward base though it lay about ten miles from the cat's lair. He and Drury/Carroll set to work cutting light but strong logs for a trap. Grizzly fastened two of the finished logs on each side of each mule and horse and one on each side of the tame grizzly. The ends of the ten-foot poles dragged on the ground behind the animals like Indian travois poles. Thus kedge-anchored, the animals made very slow progress and took half a day to reach the site which Adams chose for his trap. It lay athwart the big cat's accustomed trail, on a rocky rise within the gorge but about one-fourth mile from the inaccessible den. As soon as the rudely finished logs were unloaded, Adams sent his companion back with the animals for another load while he started to build the pen. He kept Ben, Lady Washington, the cubs, and Rambler with him for someone to talk to.

That night, he was aroused again by the roar of the beast which he sought. The cry was loud and piercing but short and clear and quite unlike the call of any puma he had ever hunted or, in fact, of any animal which he had ever heard. He was convinced that the animal was of a new and rare species, as he had first reckoned from the appearance of its firm and large paw prints. But, again, the animal did not come forward although Adams was camping without a fire so as not to disturb his prey.

Several days of monotonous labor resulted in a strong trap which Adams baited before returning to his hiding place 300 yards from the cave. His post gave him a clear, straight-line view of the trail, the trap, and the den itself in the distance. After tying Ben, Rambler and Lady Washington together, Grizzly sat down beside them and wrapped himself in a blanket like a squaw, ready to watch all night if necessary. It was the night of a new moon and the gorge was darker than the inside of a cow. The strain of watching, atop the fatigues of the last few days, overcame Grizzly's willpower and he fell asleep against Ben. However, it seemed that he had barely fallen asleep when a great roar lashed him wide awake.

Startled, Adams came to a kneeling position in his blanket and, groping automatically for his Kentucky rifle, blinked the sleep out of his eyes to try to pierce the surrounding shadows. He could see nothing along the trail but, within only a few moments, the roar was repeated, this time in a more subdued tone as if it were given by a different animal. Suddenly he saw them—three animals, apparently a mother and two cubs or kittens. In the darkness, the adult cat looked to be the size of a Bengal tiger but its coat was spotted like that of a leopard. Adams knew that he had never laid eyes on the likes of it in all his tramping over the mountains of the West. The mother crawled out of the opening of her lair and proceeded to worm her way through the jumble of rocks at the cliff's edge, disappearing and reappearing in the granitic clutter as Adams watched. She halted, turned, and apparently called to the kittens which were dawdling behind, scuffling and playing. Adams tightened his grip on the stock of his rifle, thinking that, perhaps, it would be better to shoot the mother and capture the young. But he decided to trust to his new trap so he remained as silent as a stump while the trio paraded down the trail and disappeared into the darkness.

Although he kept watch the remainder of the night, he saw nothing. However, toward dawn, he was startled from a reverie by the deeper roar of the male, which he had heard several nights earlier. He could even hear the steps of the beast but, strain his eyes as he would, he could not catch a glimpse of the "leopard." When dawn's light slanted across the opening where the trap lay, Adams examined it. He found tracks of the prowling animals circling the pen but the wily cats had given it a respectable berth, for all their curiosity.

Beginning to lose faith in the efficacy of the box trap, Grizzly decided to double his chances of success. He would dig a pit with a horizontal falling door, or lid, right on the cat's trail. The excavation which he and Drury/Carroll dug was eight feet long, six feet across, and fully ten feet deep. Grizzly Adams mounted the door on a log axle so that it would swing down with the weight of any animal of considerable size which might tread on it. Carefully removing all traces of their work, Adams covered the lid with dirt, leaves and grass to make it resemble the nearby ground as much as possible. He then hung a piece of raw mutton above the pit and retreated to his blind.

That very night, quite soon after sunset, the male jaguar—for that was what Adams decided the great cat must be—appeared. At the mouth of the den he gazed about with his cold, cruel eyes, then sniffed the air like a dog. But the savor of the mutton did not reach as far as the lair and although the cat leaped down from the cave mouth it was only to brace his front paws against a boulder and to rock back and forth, stretching and yawning away the aftereffects of a sound and long sleep. When the female appeared, she came up to her mate and licked his neck. In pure feline pleasure, the great spotted animal then rolled over and over on the ground like a housecat at play.

Finally, master and consort struck out on the trail toward Adams's blind. The male, Adams saw, was twice the size of a mountain lion and his coat, covered with dark round spots, was beautiful. Moreover, his mien was so lordly that it was a pleasure for Grizzly just to watch him pad down the path. He led his mate to the pit area but was obviously suspicious and, after smelling about the fringes of the excavation, he made a wide circuit, which the female dutifully followed. Adams's heart sank as they passed the pit, only to rise again as he saw that the lord of the chaparral was making a beeline for the trap! The jaguar examined the log pen closely with eye and nose and even entered the structure, as did his good wife, but they refused to disturb the bait and, shortly, quit the trap to vanish over a ridge nearby. Adams stayed put, right where he was, watchful all that night, but neither heard nor saw anything more of the jaguar family.

During the next several weeks, Adams replenished the bait

in his two traps, offering the most choice morsels, and even tried staking out live animals. But it was all in vain. Now and then he caught a sight of the canny animals but only fleeting glimpses. When he gave up the traps as a bad investment and settled down to stalk and shoot the parents, in order to catch the kittens, it was as if word of his change of intention had spread throughout the feline kingdom. The jaguars just disappeared. Adams never saw the majestic male again and only once stumbled on the mother and kittens. In a gorge far from their home cañon, he blundered upon them. The hunter fired and both Ben and Rambler rushed at the cat. Adams never really regretted that the male was absent, for his ball missed and the female leaped at the greyhound and grizzly as if they were cottontails. In a savage but short combat, she tore both of Grizzly's animal companions badly before making an easy escape. Hulking Ben was so worsted that Adams had to give him surgical as well as medical care during the next week. Although he remained in the area, on a constant lookout for the strange and courageous beasts which had wandered up from their range in northern Mexico, Adams never found another trace of them or of any others of their breed.

With the nip of fall in the air and that season's leafy signal flags already raining down around the bases of the deciduous trees along their way, Adams led Drury/Carroll (whom he now, forgetfully, sometimes began to call Brown!) back toward the great valley of the *tulares*. Near Tejon Pass, Adams camped again for a last fling at trapping. He used two log traps, or box traps, one with a special double door, and also another African-style pitfall, such as had failed him against the jaguars. Luck was not with him this time, either, and though he smeared the area with blood and used both fresh bait and live decoys, he got no cats. A puma invaded the double-doored trap but made its escape when one of the doors stuck in its fall.

However, one day Adams found the lion's hidden den and decided to beard the beast in its lair. "Brown," he said to Drury/Carroll/Brown, "we must have those young lions. It would be a burning shame now to go away without them."

Laughingly, his companion replied, "Ask their mother to lend them to you for a little while."

"Very good," said Grizzly, winking at his partner. "Here's my card. Tell her to take it to her bosom and she will never fear as to the care I shall take of her children." With these joshing words, Adams drew his bowie knife and made as if to hand it to his companion.

"Thank you," said his friend, who continued the joke by saying, "But when I visit the King of Beasts I want to take a *reporter* with me." And he tapped the barrel of his hunting rifle to make his point.

One Saturday morning, after sharpening their knives and laying in a supply of pine knots for torches, the two hunters checked the priming of their pieces and ascended the steep hill leading to the lion's den. Both examined the terrain carefully, suspecting that there might be another exit than the one which they had spied. But they found nothing so, after building a fire in front of the cave, they dropped to their knees and began to crawl into its mouth. Each man had his pistol in his belt, a torch in his left hand and a hunting knife and rifle, both clenched in his right fist. The dog, Rambler, followed them but the tame bears waited, at Adams's command, outside.

The den ran in a zigzag course and, unable to see but a few feet ahead, both Adams and Drury/Carroll/Brown were understandably apprehensive. But, shortly, Grizzly felt a breath of air blowing on his face and realized that there was indeed an alternate, well-hidden entrance to the den. They crept toward it but stopped when they heard a low growl succeeded by a snort.

"Brown," whispered Grizzly, "call up the dog! Here are

the beasts, sure enough, and right in front of us." Adams, as usual, could not refrain from teasing his companion, whose courage was hardly overproof. "We are in a delightful fix. We can't retreat without leaving that indignant animal to make a meal of us in the operation. We can't advance without first making a meal of her for whoever likes that kind of provender. Prepare, old boy," intoned Adams, theatrically, "to fight or die!"

The voice of his companion was an echoing quaver. "What do you advise us to do?"

"Have my courage," demanded Grizzly. "For the infernal thing will never come at us while our torches burn as brightly as they do and that is some comfort. As for the rest of the story, I'll guarantee the silence of one critter the moment I can see its eyes. The other you can take care of, surely."

Just then, the roars grew louder and Adams broke off, seeing the flash of yellow eyes in the gloom ahead. He took clumsy aim, juggling torch, knife and rifle somehow, and—involuntarily—called to his dog as he did so. At the moment his finger squeezed on the trigger, Rambler dashed into his line of vision and he relaxed. The lion, a female, shrugged off the hound's attack and seized Rambler by the throat. Adams laid his rifle aside and scuffed forward on his knees as fast as the cramped quarters of the cave would permit. He grabbed the long tail of the cat with his right hand, which still clasped the knife, shifted his grip to his left hand (still holding the torch) and struck her in the body with his bowie knife. With a scream, the cat dropped the dog and turned on Adams but the hissing torch blazing in her face caused her to draw back, grimacing and spitting her hate. Recoiling like a spring, the catamount gathered herself up and sprang for the entrance of the lair, dragging Adams who, somehow, still clung to her tail. At last, Adams's partner got a good sight on the animal and dropped her with a single shot from his pistol.

The hunters passed on out through the hidden back entrance of the cave without seeing either the male or the dead puma's kittens. Grizzly fetched new torches and they re-entered to make a very diligent and minute search and, although the male had fled, in a nest of leaves and debris Adams found five kittens. He wrapped them up in his buckskin coat. The Yankee wanted to continue examining the cave but his nervous companion urged that they get out. Adams was not worried about the male returning and tried to soothe his friend by saying, "Never fear, let him come. We are a match, my boy, for any pair of lions in California and particularly in a place like this." However, the Old Hunter saw that his words were having no good effect so he decided to humor the younger man. He ordered the exploration broken off, for a return to camp with the squirming, squealing trophies.

Back over the Tehachapis rolled the wagon and down into the San Joaquin Valley. Adams was undecided whether to winter in Corral Hollow or in the Sierra Nevada, so he postponed a decision and struck north along the foot of the Coast Range. Only a day or so beyond the Tejon his path crossed that of a party of mustangers. He joined them in several excursions after the wiry wild horses of the San Joaquin and found the animals to be in good condition. In fact, he grew to relish horse beefsteaks and laid in a good supply of dried horsemeat, as well, for future travel. Unfortunately, during one of Adams's hunting trips with the mustangers, Drury let his two horses break away and join a band of wild horses. The two mounts quickly reverted to a wild state and though Adams morosely searched the area, he had to give up without recovering them.

Proceeding north for five or six days with the mules, Adams and his followers reached Mission San Miguel on the Salinas River. They arrived at the little mission village at night, with moonlight bathing it in a peaceful and romantic illumination. Perhaps Adams was moonstruck; in any case, a series of misfortunes now beset him. They reached the river at a high hill and in the steep descent to the river, sparkling in the lunar light, the wagon overset although Drury was hanging on to a rear wheel with all his might and main. Down the slope tumbled the whole party, hell-bent for destruction. Everything was scattered helter-skelter but, miraculously, no serious damage was done.

After gathering their far-flung possessions by moonlight, the two men pushed on near dawn for the riverbank. Since the stream was slow and shallow, Adams decided to strike right across it to camp on the far side. Foolishly, Grizzly did not check the condition of the stream bed and when he stopped the mules to let them drink, the wagon's wheels sank into quicksand above their hubs. Geeing and hawing was of no avail; the wagon and team was stuck fast. The two tired men, grumbling and swearing, unhitched the mules and drove them out, then got the menagerie ashore and lastly began the laborious task of unloading all cargo from the shipwrecked wagon. By dawn's light, everything was on the bank except the vehicle itself. Since they were exhausted and the wagon was not likely to wander off, Adams and Drury/Carroll/Brown left it where it was and rolled up in their blankets for a little sleep.

The two travelers were awakened by the sound of merry laughter. They rubbed the sleep from their eyes to find themselves surrounded by a large group of people from San Miguel, mostly *Californios*. These folk made many jokes over Adams's stranding but, for once, he saw the humor of his ill luck and joined in the laughter. With the aid of several of the Spanish-Californians, expert horsemen all, he soon had the wagon free of the clutching sands of the Salinas. As he and Drury repacked the wagon bed, his visitors examined, respectfully, his captive and tame bears. They were very pleased by this break in their normal routine and they asked Grizzly and his friend to dine with them. Adams would have liked nothing better than a civilized dinner but because of the shabbiness of his greasy buckskins, he felt it necessary to decline the kind invitation.

Driving on through a now more settled country, Adams and his bears became the target of all curiosity. Some ranchers even gave him milk to feed the young animals. For some reason, this dietary change did not suit them and several died. However, Lady Washington, Ben Franklin and Rambler were all thriving, for which Grizzly was grateful. In these settled areas, there were so many dogs that Adams could no longer let his trio tag along freely in the wake of the wagon. He tied them to the vehicle for the protection of the ranchos' dogs and to avoid difficulty with dog lovers and dog owners.

After following the Salinas downstream (northward) for several days, misfortune struck again. Once again, for a third time, the wagon capsized. This time it was angling across a side hill above the river when one of the mules balked. The wagon toppled and Adams, driving, dropped the reins and jumped just in time to save himself. The wagon's tongue and bed were broken in the tumble; one of the mules, dragged down with it, was severely injured, as was a small bear; a deer and an elk were killed. With the wagon once again repaired and repacked, the party continued on the main road to San Jose. But the battered mule was so lame that they had to lay over for several days at the very first rancho they hit. Luckily, Adams found that he could be of some service to the ranchero, to repay the man's hospitality. The ranchero asked him if he could do anything about the predatory grizzly which was killing so many of his calves.

Adams examined the beast's tracks and was delighted to find that it was a big specimen—"not unworthy of the honor of a meeting." He decided to turn the corral into a great trap. After the rancher had driven all livestock out of it, leaving the body of a calf behind as bait in the center of the stockade of five-foot poles driven into the ground and lashed together with rawhide strips, Adams took up his vigil. He and Ben and Rambler hid in a pile of logs adjacent to the corral.

The night was one of beautiful moonlight and it was easy to see for considerable distances. It was about 10 P.M. when the bear appeared. Boldly and fearlessly, it marched right up to the cattle pen but there it raised its muzzle and sniffed the air many times. This performance almost persuaded Adams that the grizzly had smelled him but, no, it approached the side of the corral and leaped over it with ease. It was truly a monstrous animal so Adams did not shoot but held his fire prudently until the beast should gorge itself. However, he had great difficulty in keeping his volunteers, Ben and Rambler, in check; both the grizzly and the greyhound were itching for a fight.

After some time, Grizzly Adams crept forward to the pen. He braced his rifle on the top of the wall of pickets and fired at the spot just behind one shoulder. As the beast fell, Grizzly called to Ben and Rambler, who needed no urging. They fairly dove over the wall to do battle in the enclosure. While they milled and scrummed, Adams got another load into his long rifle and, finding an opening, snapped off another shot. But even this second wound did not stop the savage bruin. By now, the din at the corral had awakened the whole ranch and men came on the run, with their dogs. But, pre-emptorily, Adams ordered them back, for the grizzly had Rambler in his jaws and was shaking him like a rag doll although Ben was trying to distract the brute and rescue his canine chum. This time it was Adams's turn to vault the corral fence. He rushed headlong at the bear and with the momentum of his run drove his bowie knife deep into the brute's neck. Still, the monster did not succumb but, at least, it dropped Rambler to attend to Adams. One swipe of its talons tore Grizzly's buckskins off him. Now Ben—"noble Ben!"—diverted its ferocious attention and the New Englander was able to drive the blade of his knife, repeatedly, to the hilt just behind the beast's shoulder. At last the behemoth rolled over, dead.

Now, Adams called to the *Californios* to see the vanquished raider. They looked and called out their approbation: *"Muy bueno, Americano!"* Adams, as a result of his victory over "the infernal calf-killer," as they called it, was the hero of the hour. His fame spread before him up the Salinas Valley smoothing the way for his march to his destination, San Jose.

CHAPTER XV

SAN FRANCISCO'S MOUNTAINEER

IN the winter of 1855, the big, bad bears came down from the mountains with their master, for good. Now Grizzly first began regularly scheduled exhibitions of his wild animals in San Jose. This new business venture may have been as much out of necessity as inclination. Apparently, Grizzly was once again roughly handled by "civilized" folk—bankers again, if not attorneys. In 1855 San Francisco suffered a sharp business recession in which, one after the other, the major banking houses of the city failed until even the Gibraltar-like Adams and Company (no relation) went under. Scores of prominent San Franciscans, such as James King of William, were suddenly insolvent and the great number of common men pauperized included Adams. Grizzly said little about it but he did refer to it in passing, criticizing "those magnificent banking concerns whose failure . . . consumed the laborious earnings of so many small proprietors, myself among them."

From San Jose, Adams and his wild animal troupe made their way to San Francisco via the redwoods area of the Peninsula, south of the metropolis. In San Francisco, Adams's luck changed, and for the better, when he met a young reporter in September 1856 who became a good friend and booster. The journalist was Theodore H. Hittell, destined to become one of California's major historians. But at the moment, Hittell was heading up the Local News desk of the San Francisco *Daily Evening Bulletin,* the paper founded by James King of William, the martyr-editor whose murder led to the Vigilance Committee of 1856.

Hittell's interest was piqued by a small sign which Adams had posted on a door leading to the basement of 143 Clay Street, near Leidesdorff. The reporter dropped down the staircase to find himself in the midst of a close-quartered zoo. Hittell was delighted with wild Adams and his furry friends and the story they promised. Before long, he was an unpaid public relations man for the Mountaineer Museum and the Mountaineer himself. Grizzly gave him a tour of his wild beasts on that first visit, complete with the little spiel which the hunter had worked up for his cash (25 cents) customers. Hittell was amused at the patter of the crusty old mountain man turned showman—"And here is Samson, the largest grizzly bear ever caught, weighing over 1,000 pounds, and, finally, Benjamin Franklin, King of the Forest. . . ."

Adams's first San Francisco museum was modesty itself. Small wonder that his admission charge was a mere two bits. The best exhibition hall which he could afford was a large but dark and dingy basement with a low ceiling. It was reached via a flight of stairs on the south side of Clay, between Montgomery and Sansome Streets. Adams chained Ben and the Lady to bolts in the middle of the floor. There the two giants paced restlessly and endlessly in ten-foot circles determined by the unyielding, five-foot-long logging chains which fettered them. Perhaps their brute brains dreamed of the freedom of the wide open spaces which they and their master had known and which they had now quitted forever. Adams kept long hours there in the middle of the wild throng, showing the animals from ten in the morning till noon, from two to five in the afternoon, and from seven to ten at night, daily.

Now and again, Ben and Lady Washington, one or the

other, would rear up, rattle his or her chains and reverse the direction of march. Off to the side, likewise chained in place, were seven other bears, including several younger grizzlies and a cinnamon. The other bruins of the museum were common black bears. Near the front of the basement zoological garden, in an open stall, two large elk chewed their cuds. Farther back, Adams had placed a compact row of cages containing his cougars and smaller animals. Here also were a few birds, including eagles. But Hittell's eyes always returned to the monster of the bargain basement zoo—huge, hulking Samson. Nine of Adams's bears could be considered as friendly enough and content with their roles of trick performers. But ornery old Samson was pure *Ursus horribilis.* Much too dangerous to be chained out in the open like Ben or the Lady, the brute—three-fourths of a ton of muscle, fangs and claws—was penned in an iron cage. The young reporter was grateful for the stout iron bars between the monster and himself, as he looked Samson over. He noted, "From his look and actions, as well as from the care taken to rail him off from spectators, it was evident that he was not to be approached too closely." Earlier—on January 4, 1856—the *Wide West* had run an engraving on its front page showing "Some of Our First Citizens," apparently Lady Washington, her cub, Fremont, and another cub, in a great iron cage, perhaps the one in which Adams finally retained Samson while giving the rest of his troupe more freedom. The woodcut, or wood engraving, was made from a drawing by artist Charles Nahl, a friend of Hittell's who would, eventually, illustrate that writer's biography of Grizzly Adams.

Like any good reporter nosing out a story, Hittell pumped Adams and made voluminous notes on a scratch pad. He sized Grizzly up thus: "He was quite as strange as any of his animals. He was a little over medium size, muscular and wiry, with sharp features and penetrating eyes. He was apparently about fifty years of age but his hair was very gray and his beard very white. He was dressed in coat and pantaloons of buckskin, fringed at the edges and along the seams of arms and legs. On his head he wore a cap of deerskin, ornamented with a foxtail and, on his feet, buckskin moccasins."

If Hittell was awed and a little frightened by Samson, he was highly impressed with Lady Washington and Ben Franklin, Adams's closest friends, largely because of the perfect control in which their keeper held them. Adams explained the *entente cordiale* he had with Ben; the bear had twice saved his life in encounters with wild grizzlies. To show off their teeth, Adams not only placed his hands on their jaws but even right into their maws. He had them walk erect on their hind legs, "talk" (growl) on cue, and perform various other tricks. He wound up his little exhibition by having them engage in a mock boxing match with him and with each other. The reporter noted that there was nothing at all grudging about their compliance with their master's orders. They played with immense good nature, seemingly enjoying every moment of the tricks they performed.

Reporter Hittell noticed bald spots on the backs of the two tame giants. He asked Adams the reason for the worn-off hair. The Yankee told him about the bears serving him in the wilds as pack animals and regretted that he could not show him the special packsaddles which he had made. He had left them in the mountains. But, to demonstrate to his curious visitor how easily a grizzly could carry a considerable burden, he unchained Ben, climbed on his back and rode him around the room for several circuits. Then he dismounted and took up a sack of feed and threw it across the bear's back. Ben lumbered around the basement as if he had hauled grain all his life.

From this very first encounter, Grizzly and Hittell hit it off very well. They were soon the firmest of friends and the reporter featured Adams and his show in the *Evening Bulletin*. Grizzly appreciated the free publicity for his museum and read every one of the brief notices which his friend inserted in Thomas S. King's paper. The first story appeared in the October 10, 1856, issue of the *Bulletin*, on page 3. Titled "California Zoological Collection," it described the proprietor and related how perfectly this Clay Street mountaineer had domesticated and fascinated (i.e., hypnotized) his animals, up to and including the most dangerous grizzlies. Hittell volunteered that mastery over bears was much more difficult than taming lions, leopards and tigers, because the American beasts normally knew nothing of the gratitude, intelligence and affection of the Old World animals. Hittell ran over the roster of Adams's actors, listing the dead (stuffed foxes of "every" species) as well as the quick, and indicating that Grizzly was currently after a Seal Rocks sea lion to round out his collection. He advised his readers that the exhibition was well worth a visit. He did a little spadework toward a relocation of Adams's crowded menagerie, too, by suggesting that if a sufficient public patronage should develop, there would be the possibility of Adams's setting up a permanent amphitheater—that is, a zoo. Thus, said Hittell, Californians would have the rare collection preserved in San Francisco for their education and entertainment and Adams would change his avowed plan of taking the menagerie to Europe where he was confident it would attract much attention.

In his first article, Hittell, puzzled by Adams's idiosyncratic assuming and dropping of various Christian names, most of which he was not entitled to, called him simply "Mr. Adams." By the next day, Hittell—if not Adams—had settled on Grizzly's current go-by as authentic and called him William Adams when he likened him to a Californian Van Amburgh. The latter was one of the most famous animal trainers of nineteenth-century America. Born in Fishkill, New York, about 1815, Van Amburgh became a partner in a traveling menagerie company and came to be called the Lion Tamer for his mastery of the big cats.

Hittell really waxed enthusiastic over the mountain man, now, saying that his command over the wild animals was absolutely astonishing—"One of the most complete examples of the power of man over the ordinarily savage denizens of the forest." Next, the reporter passed on some tidbits of mountain lore which he had picked up in his interview with Adams. He exploded the idea that the wild grizzly hugged its victims to death, for example, repeating what Adams had told him—that the beast which walked like a man preferred to clasp its prey around the shoulders and then to gnaw away at the neck. As for the folklore about mountain lions attacking humans, he learned from Grizzly that this would occur only when one of the big tom cougars was suffering from intense hunger.

The reporter called Lady Washington a Victoria bear, or Russian bear, not a grizzly, because Adams told him that he had lassoed her north of Oregon in 1854. With typical journalistic license, Hittell converted Washington Territory into Russian Alaska. He also mentioned how the Lady liked to tote Adams's camp kettles and other utensils about on her back. Of the biggest bear, Hittell had this to say: "Samson swings his unwieldly weight and jumps about quite briskly at his master's orders. He is said to be tolerably tame and very obedient but as a matter of prudent precaution, is confined in a large cage."

According to the writer, only one live animal in the museum had not been caught by Adams himself. The one exception was the two-year-old, 175-pound cougar which was captured in 1855 while swimming the Columbia River near Portland. After being pursued by the steamer *Belle,* the catamount had been lassoed and hoisted from the river. (There was another exception which Hittell did not mention, the only tame animal in the collection. This was the State Fair Hog—the 800-pound, prize-winning pig of the California State Fair. Adams had secured the immense porker in San

Jose, where the Fair was held in October of that year, but probably did not as yet have the animal on exhibit when Hittell wrote his piece.)

On October 17, Hittell featured Ben Franklin on pages one and two of the *Bulletin,* describing the two-and-a-half-year-old, 800-pound friend of Rambler as Adams's favorite, thanks to the "Fight Of His Life," near Strawberry Lake, in the spring of 1855 when Adams's short command, "St'e, boy!" (Steady, boy), had caused young Ben to fight shoulder to shoulder with his master against his own savage kin. Their antagonist, a huge female, not only scarred Ben's muzzle permanently but also punched a hole the size of a silver dollar near the top of his master's forehead. It was a fight which Adams would never forget and which would, eventually, be the death of him.

Thomas S. King's *Bulletin* was not the only daily to see a good story in the Wild Yankee. The then-monarch of the dailies, the San Francisco *Daily Alta California,* on October 21, 1856, wrote up Adams's Mountaineer Museum, calling attention to the fact that Lady Washington was not as well-mannered as was Ben. "The Russian bear is, by turns, very savage and cannot be commanded like the grizzly, Ben Franklin." (One wonders if the *Alta* reporter confused belli-cose Samson with Lady Washington.) The *Alta* correspondent appeared to be as eager as Theodore Hittell to help Grizzly's business and he hastily added a reassuring note, "But all is conducted with decorum."

Doubtless this zeal in favor of Adams's zoo was as much a matter of vested interest as it was genuine Fourth Estate *noblesse oblige.* For Grizzly had just begun, that very day, to run paid advertisements for his establishment in the *Alta.* He also threw some advertising business to the *Bulletin,* of course, to repay Hittell, in part, for his kindness. But, in any case, the *Alta* was delighted with the Clay Street eccentric: "He has been some years in the mountains and encountered many hardships and dangers in capturing the monsters now in his collection. . . . His celebrated bear, Ben Franklin, is a perfect wonder in his way. His keeper mounts him and gives him an invitation to shake him off. Bruin stands on three legs and rolls like an elephant but when this method fails he throws back his paws and claws his rider down. He stands up on his hind legs and his keeper gives him a gentle shove and over and over and over he goes as if impelled by an irresistible force. This animal weighs 800 pounds and, in the mountains, hunts with his master and is very eager for game. Buchanan and Fremont, two bears, are curiosities in their way. Both are polite bears and don't dishonor their namesakes." (Apparently, Adams thought too little of Millard Fillmore, the ex-President and other major candidate in 1856, to name a grizzly after him.)

Adams was so pleased with his growing fame that he decided to capitalize on it by invading a new field—the theater. Or, better, the circus and theater. Perhaps Grizzly first met Joe Rowe at the California State Fair, October 7–10, 1856, when Adams picked up his rather ludicrous pig to add to his otherwise wild family. Joesph Rowe, California's pioneer circus entrepreneur, put on a show there at the Fair in a modern and much-touted "Water-proof Pavilion—Impervious to Rain." There is little chance that Adams exhibited his bears at the Fair since neither the records of the Fair itself, the San Francisco papers, the San Jose *Tribune,* nor the *Telegraph* and *Register* of the last-named city mention it.

But, on Monday, October 27, Colonel Rowe was back in San Francisco to open his Pioneer Circus. His November 1st advertisement in the *Herald* (located right above Adams's museum ad, incidentally), headlined the German Brothers, apparently an equestrian act featured by the circus. Where Adams intoned, "The proprietor has just returned from the mountains with the largest collection of wild animals ever exhibited on the Pacific Coast . . ." Rowe was bragging of the

benefits for the spectator of his bringing a circus into a legit-
imate theater. He dwelt on the horsemanship, the pageantry,
which he would introduce to San Francisco's theatergoers.
He opened at the Union Theater, on Commercial Street between Kearney and Dupont (now Grant), a jinxed house
which changed its name a half-dozen times as its prestige
sagged and which ended as a Chinese opera house. Rowe had
it remodeled into a hippodrome for his Pioneer Circus.

November 2, 1856, was described as a quiet Sabbath by the
San Francisco *Herald*. The city was so quiet, in fact, that not
one arrest was made by the police during the entire day and
night! But it also marked the debut of Grizzly Adams as a
thespian of sorts. He trod the boards of the Union Theater
as he and Rowe, briefly, merged their careers. The next day
saw a packed house at the Union Amphitheater or Hippodrome, as the Union Theater was now called, for people
flocked to see Rowe's grizzled new performer and his pets.
The *Alta California* reported on the new star: "A valuable
addition has lately been made to the circus in the person of
Mr. Adams, bear hunter, who appears with a couple of bears
in what is called 'The Pony Races.' " Adams probably participated in the remaining 7:30 performances of Rowe's short
season until the Colonel bundled his regulars aboard Captain Stott's bark, *Francis Palmer,* early in November to sail
for Honolulu and, he fondly hoped, a repeat of the triumphal
tour of his circus to Australia and the South Seas in 1852–
1854. According to the press, the entire circus (except for
Rowe's agent, J. B. Rochette) sailed, but apparently Adams
decided to pass up the Sandwich Islands. He continued his
regular advertisements for the museum and the *Alta* ran a
brief item on November 6: "You that have not seen the wonderful collection of animals at No. 143 Clay Street, go and
see them. Mr. Adams, who has there the most perfect control
over the bears in his exhibition, has a number of other
curiosities which are well worthy [of] the attention of the

curious." Exactly one month later, the *Bulletin* ran a new ad, describing his new headquarters in the California Exchange.

One day in late 1856, Adams met George Washington Call and made another good friend. Call was a twenty-seven-year-old Ohioan who had come overland to the mines in 1852 but who had ended up on California's Redwood Coast, prospering in Humboldt Bay's logging industry. In 1855 Call had left Humboldt County to come to San Francisco. After their Frisco meeting, Adams and Call came to an agreement whereby Call furnished the Old Hunter with enough money to transfer his museum to adequate quarters in the California Exchange on the corner of Clay and Kearney streets. Receipts, thanks to the newspaper publicity and better location, grew and Adams's fame began to spread. Eventually, since expenses remained high on such trenchermen as the grizzlies and elk, Call decided to withdraw from the business, but for two years he stuck with Adams as his partner and financial agent. (He was, probably, the real owner of the museum.) In 1858 the Buckeye pulled out and traveled until 1872 when he finally returned to California to settle on a ranch at Salt Point, near the old Russian outpost of Fort Ross.

The California Exchange, with its entrance at street level on Clay, was a far better site than the basement. Adams fitted up the much more spacious first floor allotted him into a showroom and renamed his establishment the Pacific Museum, though people came to call it the California Menagerie. As before, he lived right with his animals, sleeping on a bearskin or buffalo robe in a corner of the exhibit hall itself or in an adjoining chamber when he wanted a little privacy. Although profits came to him along with fame, he never traded his rough frontier garb for serge and broadcloth, and he cut quite a figure in colorful San Francisco, as he strode along Kearney Street in his buckskins, even when unaccompanied by his bearish partners. His one concession to civilized life was abandoning his frying pan. He occasionally cooked his own meals but, mostly, he preferred to dine out at one or another of San Francisco's many excellent restaurants.

With more room and more money—although the latter tended to leak through his fingers quickly—Adams added several new attractions to his menagerie after he moved to the California Exchange. He took on an antelope, a rattlesnake, and a sea lion which became quite famous in New York after Adams let Barnum grubstake him. But the clown of the little zoo remained the clumsy, ludicrous, Rocky Mountain white bear (really a grizzly, too) named Funny Joe. Though two years old, he was as playful and humorous as a monkey, sitting, standing, dancing and taking the arms of visitors, to swing along beside them like a lady friend, then to tumble in somersaults before begging some tobacco to chew or a cigar to smoke.

Adams grouped several of the other bears to form the Happy Family. One of them was George, the so-called hyena bear of Washington Territory. With his long forelegs, he was easily the fastest runner of the whole bear clan. Adams never saw as fast a bear in his entire life. But George also had a nasty temper, at times, and was not really tamed. When Hittell first visited Grizzly Adams, Grizzly was lame and limping from a bite by the vicious beast. The others of the family circle were of sunnier dispositions, whether the Sierra cinnamon or the very tame and playful little Buchanan. Most good-natured of all was Lady Washington's cub, Fremont, or Young Fremont. Hittell was particularly taken with this ball of fur, feeling that he was destined to be the eventual star of the whole show, prophesying, "He shall be the President of the Collection!"

The reporters passed over the bald eagles and gray eagles without comment and Adams apparently never secured a live California condor. But they mentioned that Adams had broken his two elk to both saddle and harness. Grizzly had several smaller animals of interest, such as those described by the press as "cats or martins" with sweeping zoological inaccuracy. One tiny fellow (perhaps a weasel-like fisher) with a long bushy tail, though gentle as a house cat, was far superior to any tom as a rat catcher. In their several stories, Hittell and the other journalists continued to depict the museum as an interesting exhibition and one of value both in terms of instruction and amusement.

Adams's receipts, at two bits a head, were never so great that he could run more than a modest advertisement in the daily press. Nor did he often change the format or copy, preferring to keep costs down. After his December 1856 move to the California Exchange, he had to abandon the old ad which had done such yeoman work for business at 143 Clay. So the December 8 *Bulletin* ran a piece about how docile and skillful were the performing bears, now relocated, and the next day the *Alta* came through with a paraphrase of the *Bulletin* and, undoubtedly, Adams's handout. But the *Alta* added, "The rooms [in the California Exchange] have been very conveniently fitted up, and, as the price of admission is fixed at only 25 cents, there is no doubt that crowds will be attracted to witness so great and so many rare specimens of Natural History."

Adams now settled down to three solid years of showmanship in San Francisco, mostly in his museum but with occasional forays onto the boards of local theaters. Between July 1857 and December 1859, he told his adventures to Theodore Hittell. The reporter would come to the museum most afternoons after the *Bulletin* was put to bed. He took notes on everything that Grizzly said, intending to write a book, autobiographical in format, on Grizzly and his life of adventure. The mountain man was both flattered and pleased. He would talk for an hour or two, with many interruptions caused by museum customers. His amanuensis recalled: "I told him plainly that I wanted nothing except the truth and he assured me that he would give it." Apparently, the reporter never dreamed just how difficult it was for a rugged mountain man to wrestle only with truths without pinning down an occasional half-truth or untruth. But the bear tamer satisfied Hittell, who said, "On various occasions I cross-questioned him sharply; but his replies were always satisfactory and, I believe, truthful. His memory seemed remarkably good." In this last respect, Hittell was quite correct. Adams had a memory as unfading as an amaranth but, like Jim Bridger or Jim Beckwourth, he simply could not resist adding fanciful arabesques to the bare outlines of fact which almost total recall produced.

Grizzly made a major reappearance, theatrically, either late in 1857 or early in 1858 at Tom Maguire's beautiful Opera House. It was on November 28, 1856, that the illiterate Irish dandy opened his dazzling theater. It boasted a great orchestra pit and a thirty-five-foot-deep stage. The curtain bore a magnificent view of Venice with canals, domes, ships and gondolas. Gaslit throughout, the house's interior was dominated by a huge chandelier of twenty burners depending from the domed roof. The private boxes were ornamented with gilt moldings and rich hangings of gold and crimson—all in most striking contrast to the worn buckskins of Adams, onstage. Grizzly was a featured performer in this luxurious opera house. His last night, a benefit, was on January 10, 1858. He was back behind the footlights again from August 20th to the 30th of that year, appearing this time at the short-lived, unlucky Lyceum Theater which, built in 1858, burned in 1860. He billed himself as Yankee Adams now, which solved the problem of deciding which of various Christian names was his own. (One area in which his elephantine memory was overtaxed.)

January 1858 ushered in no happy new year for Adams. Ben Franklin took sick from some unknown cause and refused to eat or drink for a week. He died on Sunday evening,

January 17. The press noted the passing of Adams's closest friend and the *Bulletin* produced an impressive obituary on the 19th, titled "Death of a Distinguished Californian." This was apparently written by Hittell. The piece gave a brief *vita* of Ben, from his capture as a cub by Adams near the headwaters of the Merced in 1854 to his adulthood as a wise, affectionate, tame and gentle friend of his tamer. Hittell saluted this bear which twice saved Adams's life and which bore on head and neck the scars of the battles, not to forget an injured eye, to prove his valor and loyalty. The reporter ended his obit thus: "During frequent visits to observe, over and over again, and study the habits and characteristics of his wonderful animals, we never once heard Adams express any other but sentiments of preference for this faithful creature. . . . The Old Hunter would willingly have lost all the balance of his collection to have saved Ben."

Adams was much affected by Ben's death. After that sad event he was deeply depressed for a long period of time. In August 1859 he moved his menagerie from the California Exchange to the Pavilion building, on the site of the later, famed hostelry, the Lick House. There he continued to entertain thousands of San Franciscans and visitors to the city with his wild animal show.

Probably because his purse was as gaunt and wrinkled as when he had first hit San Francisco in 1856, Adams decided in the winter of 1859 to light out for greener pastures. On January 7, 1860, he sailed with his animals on the clipper *Golden Fleece* for New York. By the time he arrived in New York harbor, Adams was a very sick man. As is often the case with Grizzly Adams, stories tend to differ, but it is certain that he was unwell and not from *mal de mer*. According to one account, in a severe struggle on shipboard with a grizzly made refractory by the change of regimen necessitated by the voyage, the old wound in his head was torn open. In New York, Adams consulted a doctor about his inflamed wound.

He was feverish and the doctor did not give him long to live.

The second version, with so much detail and therefore somewhat more likely, was vouched for by James M. Hutchings, the pioneer publisher and exploiter of Yosemite. The Englishman-turned-Californian wrote in *Hutching's Illustrated California Magazine* that Adams, whom he called "the Rocky Mountain Bear Trapper," had called at San Francisco's College of Physicians and Surgeons to see if his head could be repaired. He explained to the awestruck doctors that he had been scalped by a grizzly and, pulling off his furry cap, he showed where the wild she-grizzly had laid open his skull. According to Adams, the surgeons and Hutchings, one of the bears chained and strapped in the museum had reinjured his head with a blow. As a result, his skull, stripped of scalp and even periosteum, or bone covering, at the point of injury, had appeared to granulate. It looked, too, as if a fungus had attacked it. But this horrible condition was not the worst of it. As the English-Californian editor put it, "The end of Adams's ill luck was not yet. A few months ago he was training a monkey, which creature sprang upon the unfortunate man's head and inserted his carnivorous teeth into the wounded part. Under these combined misfortunes, Adams has lost his health and has become a great sufferer. Anyone who witnesses the pale man going through the daily training with his huge bears can easily see that his end cannot be far away. One who saw him at the College of Physicians and Surgeons states that when the heart beats, if the head is uncovered, the pulsations can be seen in the boneless portion of his cranium. We believe that no remedies can be relied on for a cure."

But Hutchings, like so many others, was putting Adams's name in the obituary column a little prematurely. That whang-leather-tough mountain man had plans which he intended to carry out in New York and he went right ahead with them. In the meantime, his fame was spreading wider and wider. Hittell's biography—or Adams's autobiography via Theodore Hittell—was published as *The Adventures of James Capen Adams, Mountaineer and Grizzly Bear Hunter of California* by Towne and Bacon of San Francisco in 1860. Later in the year a Boston edition was published. Although Hittell felt that the Civil War and other factors kept it from being the success it might have been, the book was popular and was reprinted in 1911, 1912 and 1926.

Hittell's book was well received in Adams's old hometown, San Francisco. The *Hesperian* in August 1860 reviewed it favorably, as did *Hutching's Illustrated California Magazine,* which also paid it the compliment of running excerpts and some of Charles Nahl's fine illustrations. Hutchings was high on the book, saying, "We hope that every person who has read this exceedingly brief and imperfect epitome [in the *Magazine*] will possess himself of the volume, for we can assure him it is our opinion that he will read its three hundred and seventy-eight pages with unflagging attention." In a sort of postscript, James Hutchings recalled the Clay Street mountaineer, a curiosity greater than anything in his menagerie, in the Englishman's opinion. "Adams was no common, every-day character.... His large, grizzled beard, his quaint yet expressive features; his peculiar tone of voice; his oddly fashioned garments, his easy self-possession when 'stirring up' the animals; his remarkable influence over them."

CHAPTER XVI

BUCKSKINS ON BROADWAY

ON March 17, 1860, Phineas T. Barnum, America's greatest showman of all time, bounced back from bankruptcy to repurchase his American Museum from Butler and Greenwood, to whom he had been forced to sell it when assailed by debts. He renovated the building and trimmed it with colorful flags and streamers. Posters screamed BARNUM'S ON HIS FEET AGAIN! from pillars and brick walls all over New York.

Just about a month later, Grizzly Adams arrived in New York after three and a half months at sea. Almost immediately, he set up his California Menagerie at 13th Street and Fourth Avenue. Not long after, Barnum bought a half interest in Adams's menagerie from a gentleman who claimed to be Grizzly's partner in the venture. Adams protested that he was not, that the man had simply advanced him money. However, since the fellow had passed over to Barnum a bill of sale for one-half the menagerie, it was easy for the showman to persuade Adams to accept him as an equal partner. The supposedly moribund mountaineer got along with Barnum just fine, and the showman was greatly impressed with the gentleman in buckskins who still called himself James Capen Adams, though that was his brother's name. Barnum felt that he was meeting an extraordinary man, in fact a "character." As the New Yorker said of him, "He was

213

brave and with this bravery there was enough of the romantic in his nature to make him a real hero. .... He acquired a recklessness which, added to his natural, invariable courage, rendered him one of the most striking men of the age." And, in his buckskins decorated with animals' tails, and the showy hunting cap which he had fashioned of a wolf's head (to replace a more prosaic one of deer and rabbit skins), he was, in Barnum's words, "quite as much of a show as his beasts."

According to Barnum, Adams arrived with twenty or thirty grizzlies and other bears. This is possible, but not likely. (And Barnum sometimes elasticized the truth a little, of course.) He probably had the eight or nine animals which he had exhibited in San Francisco, plus all the other beasts. Barnum made a point of mentioning Old Neptune, the sea lion which had come from San Francisco's Seal Rocks.

During their conversation, Adams doffed his lupine cap to show Barnum his head wound. The bug-eyed Barnum examined his visitor's skull. He found it, quite literally, broken in, with a portion of the brain showing. He could not help asking Adams if it was not a dangerous—indeed, a fatal—wound.

"Yes," admitted Grizzly, "that will fix me out. It had nearly healed, but old Fremont opened it for me for the third or fourth time before I left California and he did his business so thoroughly I'm a used-up man. However," he added, coolly, "I reckon I may live six months or a year, yet."

Adams continued, "Mr. Barnum, I am not the man I was five years ago. Then I felt able to stand the hug of any grizzly living and was always glad to encounter, single-handed, any sort of an animal that dared present himself. But I have been beaten to a jelly, torn almost limb from limb and nearly chawed up and spit out by these treacherous grizzly bears. However, I am good for a few months yet and, by that time, I hope we shall gain enough to make my old woman comfortable, for I have been absent from her some years."

The two men discussed how they would handle the business and it was decided that Barnum would provide a tent and manage the shows while Adams would handle all the animals. Barnum secured his big top and erected it on the later site of Wallach's Theater. Adams's wife—his "old woman" whom he had not seen for a decade or so—came from Massachusetts to New York to nurse him. Dr. Johns dressed his reopened head wound every day but told him that he would never recover and, in fact, would be in his grave in a few weeks. Adams snorted his refusal to accept the sawbones' timetable. He handled the beasts magnificently. No spectator ever suspected that the rough-looking mountain man was suffering intense pain from his broken skull and a fevered system.

On the opening day of their new joint enterprise, Grizzly paraded down Broadway and up the Bowery with his animals, behind a band. Adams led his troupe, riding on a wagon platform with three of his grizzlies. Whereas the other bears were caged, these three were not. Two were chained but the third, General Fremont, was not and Adams rode on his back.

Barnum commissioned Wynkoop, Hallenbeck and Thomas, of 113 Fulton Street, to print a 53-page pamphlet autobiography to spread Adams's fame wider and deeper in the East. The ten-cent booklet, with its printed yellow covers, was titled *Life of J. C. Adams, Known as Old Adams, Old Grizzly Adams, Containing a Truthful Account of His Bear Hunts, Fights With Grizzly Bears, Hairbreadth Escapes in the Rocky and Nevada Mountains, and the Wilds of the Pacific Coast.* It did the trick and New Yorkers flocked to the California Menagerie. Supposedly written by Old Adams himself (with no mention of a ghost writer), it bore a prefatory note by Adams guaranteeing its authenticity: "I narrate in these pages the truth without exaggeration or embellishment, as I am indifferent to idle notoriety. I flatter myself that I am too well-known among the hunters of the Rocky Mountains and the Sierra Nevada to need boasting upon my part, and the admiration of those who, not being hunters, cannot appreciate the perils of a wild beast pursuit in the wilderness, could scarcely afford much gratification to a man like myself."

Perhaps it takes one to know one. In any case, Barnum correctly sized up Adams as a tall tale teller who liked to brag that he had been everywhere and seen or done everything. So the New Yorker decided to humbug his know-it-all partner. He paid $10 for a pair of pigeons from a German chemist who had mastered a process by which he could dye birds any desired color. Indeed, he offered to supply P. T. Barnum with rainbow-colored birds if he liked. But Barnum preferred to purchase a pair of golden-hued pigeons. He labeled them GOLDEN PIGEONS FROM CALIFORNIA and sent them to Mr. Taylor, in charge of his aviary at the American Museum. He was sure that Adams would notice them on one of his frequent trips to the museum.

Barnum was a shrewd judge of men. Grizzly fell right into his trap. Not only did he visit the museum and examine the birds—pronounced excessively rare by Monsieur Guillaudeu, the naturalist and taxidermist there, since (naturally) they were unknown to Cuvier, Linnaeus, Goldsmith and Audubon—but Adams affected to be quite familiar with the breed back in California. Even better, from Barnum's point of view, Adams sought him out quickly and demanded the birds. "Mr. Barnum, you must let me have those California pigeons."

"But," said Barnum, "I can't spare them."

"But you *must* spare them," insisted Grizzly. "All the birds and animals from California ought to be together. You own half of my California Menagerie and you must lend me those birds!"

P. T. tried to calm the excited Adams. "Mr. Adams, they are too rare and valuable a bird to be hawked about in that manner."

"Oh, don't be a fool," retorted Adams. "Rare bird, indeed! Why, they are just as common in California as any other pigeon! I could have brought a hundred of them from San Francisco if I had thought of it."

Barnum continued to tease him. "But, why did you not think of it?" he asked with a suppressed smile.

"Because they are so common there. I did not think they would be a curiosity here. I have eaten them in pigeon pies hundreds of times and have shot them by the thousands."

Swallowing hard, Barnum was able to keep himself from bursting with laughter. "Oh, well, Mr. Adams, if they really are so common in California, you had better take them and you may write over and have half a dozen pairs sent to me for the museum."

"All right," said Adams, "I will send over to a friend in San Francisco and you shall have them in a couple of months."

Barnum told Adams that he would have to change the labels to read "Golden Pigeons From Australia," for reasons which he could not reveal at that moment. Still taken in, Adams agreed, saying, "Well, I will call them what you like. I suppose they are probably about as plenty in Australia as they are in California."

Two months later, the birds, now at the California Menagerie, began to look awfully mottled. Their feathers, growing out, were white at the base. Adams was so busy with his bruins that he did not notice their piebald plumage but Barnum did, and he called his partner's attention to the transformation in the birds. "Mr. Adams, I fear you will lose your Golden Pigeons. They must be very sick. I observe they are turning pale."

Astonished, Adams looked at them and immediately sized up the true situation. He turned on P. T. indignantly, and shouted, "Blast the Golden Pigeons! You had better take them back to the museum. You can't humbug me with your painted pigeons!"

Barnum laughed till he cried at the vexed look on the bearded face of his partner.

Six weeks after the California Menagerie opened, Dr. Johns advised his patient to sell out his share of it and get his worldly affairs in shape, since he was not to live much longer. "I shall live a good deal longer than you doctors think!" swore Adams. But finally he went to Barnum and said, "Mr. Barnum, you must buy me out." He named his price for half of the wild animal show and Barnum accepted. But Adams doggedly insisted on going ahead with their plans for a summer traveling circus to tour Connecticut and Massachusetts. He got Barnum to hire him as animal trainer at $60 a week, plus the expenses of his wife and himself. Barnum said that he would be glad to do so, but advised him to go ahead and rest, instead, reminding him, "You are growing weaker every day and, at best, cannot stand it more than a fortnight."

"What will you give me extra if I will travel and exhibit the bears every day for ten weeks?" asked Adams eagerly.

"Five hundred dollars," said Barnum, with a laugh.

"Done!" came back Adams. "I will do it, so draw up an agreement to that effect, at once. But mind you, draw it payable to my wife, for I may be too weak to attend to business after the ten weeks are up, and if I perform my part of the contract, I want her to get the $500 without any trouble."

When Barnum was finished with the contract, Adams snatched it up, whooping, "You have lost your $500! I am bound to live and earn it."

Barnum replied, sincerely, "I hope you may, with all my heart, and a hundred years more if you deserve it." But his words chased Adams's back out of the door as the mountain man left, chortling in high spirits for having put one over on Phineas T. Barnum—"Call me a fool if I don't earn the $500!"

Barnum dropped in on Adams's Wild West show at Hartford a fortnight later and said, "Adams, you seem to stand it pretty well. I hope you and your wife are comfortable?"

"Yes," answered Adams, "and you may as well try to be comfortable, too, for your $500 is a goner."

"All right," said Barnum. "I hope you grow better every day."

But Adams's health worsened. His face grew paler and his eyes glassy. His hands trembled. But he did not lose his nerve or his drive. After another three weeks, Barnum saw him at New Bedford. The Californian looked terrible, as if he could not live out the week. But he only complained of the New England summer's heat. "This hot weather is pretty bad for me. But my ten weeks are half expired and I am good for your $500 and, probably, a month or two longer."

The old mountain man, a wreck of his former self, said this with touching bravado. It was as if his boast were a bet which he was placing on his own life. Barnum was sorry for him and offered to pay him half of the agreed sum immediately if he would go home and rest. Adams declined to compromise.

When Barnum saw him during the ninth week of his tour, at Boston, the wan Californian was chuckling over his certain triumph although he was too weak to lead the bears into their tricks. Barnum congratulated him on his pluck and his almost-certain success. He stayed in Boston until the final, tenth week was completed, then handed Adams his $500.

Grizzly, with a grin of great satisfaction, said, "I'm sorry you're a teetotaler. I'd like to stand treat."

Just before Adams and the circus and bears had left New York on the summer tour, Barnum had paid $150 for a hunting shirt of beaverskin similar to Adams's rough garb. He intended the beautiful jacket for Herr Driesbach, the German who was to succeed Grizzly as animal trainer. Adams had used it several times during the ten-week tour, for special shows at fairs or whenever his own worn and soiled suit did not seem appropriate to the occasion. Now he said, "Mr. Barnum, I suppose you are going to give me this new hunting dress?"

"Oh, no," answered Barnum. "I got that for your successor, who will exhibit the bears tomorrow. Besides, you have no possible use for it."

"Now, don't be mean," growled Adams. "Lend me the dress if you won't give it to me, for I want to wear it home to my native village."

Barnum could not refuse. "Well, Adams, I will lend you the dress. But you will send it back to me?"

"Yes, when I have done with it," answered the mountaineer. "Now, Barnum, you have made a good thing out of the California Menagerie and so have I. But you will make a heap more. So, if you won't give me this new hunter's dress, just draw a little writing, and sign it, saying that I may wear it until I have done with it."

Barnum, thinking Adams had only a few days to live, decided to humor him. He signed the agreement.

With glee, and a broad grin, Adams exclaimed, "Come, Old Yankee, I've got you this time—see if I haven't!"

"All right, my dear fellow," smiled Barnum, "the longer you live the better I like it."

Adams went to Neponset where his wife and daughter lived. He took to bed and never left it again, alive. On the fifth day on that sickbed, the doctor said that he would not live until morning. He took it calmly but asked to be buried in Barnum's beaverskin jacket. He was not yet finished with it! The wasted face framed with gray hairs broke into a grin as he thought how he would once again get even with Barnum for fooling him with the gilded pigeons.

Calling to his wife, he reminded her about the fine coat. "Barnum agreed to let me have it until I have done with it and I am determined to fix his flint this time. He shall never see that dress again!"

Adams then talked to the local clergyman in his rough way but with such good New England grammar that the parson was surprised. He admitted having told many tall tales about his bears but he swore that he had always tried to do the straight thing in all his dealings with men. He was no church-goer, Adams admitted to the sky pilot, at least not in the normal sense. But he added, "I have attended preaching every day, Sundays and all, for the last six years. Sometimes an old grizzly gave me the sermon, sometimes it was a panther; often it was the thunder and lightning, the tempest, or the hurricane on the peaks of the Sierra Nevada or in the gorges of the Rocky Mountains, but whatever preached to me, it always taught me the undying majesty of the Creator and revealed to me the undying and unchanging love of our kind Father in Heaven. Although I am a pretty rough customer, I fancy my heart is in about the right place and I look with confidence for that rest which I so much need and which I never enjoyed upon earth."

That day, either October 25 (according to his tombstone) or the 28th, according to the family genealogist, A. N. Adams, he rested after his long say, prayed with the preacher briefly, took his hand and thanked him for his kindness. He said good-bye and was gone in an hour. But before he died he showed, by his last words, that he was still the crusty old California mountaineer, who had twice gotten the best of P. T. Barnum, for he muttered, "Won't Barnum open his eyes when he finds I have humbugged him by being buried in his new hunting dress!"

The telegraph carried news of the mountain man's death and *Harper's Weekly* on November 10 carried a brief salute to the departed bear catcher in its "Domestic Intelligence" column. It repeated the fiction of his early Aroostook childhood and transported him to California at age forty-three (1848) where he hunted wild animals in the mountains for a full decade. "His tastes led him to cultivate the society of bears," said *Harper's*, "which he did at great personal risk but with remarkable success, using them as packhorses, by day, as blankets by night, as companions at all times." The obituary concluded with a reminiscence of Adams as a New Yorker: "Few of our city readers have not seen the strange old man taking a morning airing with a bear or two, accompanied by a limited but noisy band, composed of a bass drum and a piccolo flute. He had frequent personal encounters with his bears and, after a time, people began to feel a want of something in their daily paper if the chronicle narrated not how Old Adams had lost a leg, an arm or part of his head on the day before, through the petulance of his chief grizzly. The gray-bearded, sharp-eyed, rough old hunter finally, however, succumbed to his destiny. He could conquer the passing obstinacy or ugliness of his animals but the strife left its marks and repeated attacks of bears were, at last, too much for him. Almost for the first time in his life, he spent the closing hours of his pilgrimage in the quiet repose of a civilized country home, dying with his friends."

Actually, of course, Adams, in Neponset, died far away from his truest friends—Lady Washington, Fremont, Funny Joe, even Samson and the other "critters" of his Happy Family at the California Menagerie.

Grizzly Adams was buried at Charlton, Massachusetts, under a stone which helped to straighten out some of the kinks and knots in the web of his vital statistics, although few historians or biographers have heeded the inscription. The five-foot-high gravestone, two feet wide, decorated with the carved effigy of a man and his tamed grizzly bear, gives Grizzly's true name—John Adams. His age is set at forty-eight years and his death date at October 25, 1860. Graven on the tombstone is a poetic epitaph to the man from Medway, Massachusetts, who had a score more adventures than the

most daring hero in the books of his fellow townsman, Oliver
Optic:

> And silent now the hunter lays
> Sleep on, brave tenant of the wild
> Great Nature owns her simple child
> And Nature's God to whom alone
> The secret of the heart is known
> In silence whispers that his work is done.